Turning the Page

Turning the Page

The Ultimate Guide for Teachers to Multicultural Literature

Rachel Slaughter

ROWMAN & LITTLEFIELD
Lanham • Boulder • New York • London

Published by Rowman & Littlefield
An imprint of The Rowman & Littlefield Publishing Group, Inc.
4501 Forbes Boulevard, Suite 200, Lanham, Maryland 20706
www.rowman.com

6 Tinworth Street, London, SE11 5AL, United Kingdom

British Library Cataloguing in Publication Information Available

Library of Congress Cataloging-in-Publication Data

Names: Slaughter, Rachel, 1967– author.
Title: Turning the page: the ultimate guide for teachers to multicultural literature /
    Rachel Slaughter.
Description: Lanham: Rowman & Littlefield, 2021. | Includes bibliographical references
    and index. | Summary: "Turning the Page: The Ultimate Guide for Teachers to
    Multicultural Literature helps educators find multicultural books for the classroom
    that align with the curriculum. Inside the book are a peer-reviewed metric that shows
    teachers how to substitute biased books with multicultural literature, book reviews,
    and lesson plans for multicultural books."—Provided by publisher.
Identifiers: LCCN 2020044781 (print) | LCCN 2020044782 (ebook) |
    ISBN 9781475857634 (cloth) | ISBN 9781475857641 (paperback) |
    ISBN 9781475857658 (epub)
Subjects: LCSH: Children's literature—Study and teaching—United States. |
    Multicultural education—United States | Children—Books and reading—
    United States.
Classification: LCC PN1008.8 .S53 2021 (print) | LCC PN1008.8 (ebook) |
    DDC 370.1170973—dc23
LC record available at https://lccn.loc.gov/2020044781
LC ebook record available at https://lccn.loc.gov/2020044782

To Warren T. Slaughter Jr. and Chelsea and Sadie, a.k.a. the Junior Slaughters, with love, from my heart and soul.

Contents

Foreword   ix

Preface   xi

Acknowledgments   xiii

1   Diversity in the Classroom: A Glimpse into the Changing Classroom   1

2   Adopting a Multicultural Education Program   5

3   Critical Literacy and Multicultural Literature   13

4   Generating a List of Multicultural Books   19

5   Creating a Task Force   23

6   The Multicultural Summer Reading List   27

7   The Task Force Meets Resistance and Bias   33

8   How to Normalize Multiculturalism   37

9   The Key Takeaways   47

10   The Reading QUILT Book Reviews and Lesson Plans   63

Appendix A   89

Appendix B   93

References   115

Index   127

About the Author   131

Foreword

Converse with any middle school teacher and you will immediately appreciate the arduous undertaking to locate high-quality literature attractive to adolescent students from diverse backgrounds. While there has been some advancement in regard to the publication of multicultural young adult books, the current criteria indicating the guiding principles of exemplary all-inclusive tests still remain questionable.

Moreover, while providing diverse middle school students with a plethora of high-quality multicultural texts exemplifies a progression toward ethnic literacy inclusiveness, middle school teachers are simultaneously challenged to increase their own instructional knowledge regarding exceptional culturally diverse literature.

Today's middle school settings are characterized by a significant emphasis being placed on students' standardized test scores, which have a minimal impact on erasing inequities and racism in our society. Fundamentally, however, the amalgamation of exemplary multicultural juvenile literature and competent teacher knowledge creates a classroom that can potentially motivate young adults' literacy learning and appreciation of culture diversity in our world.

Turning the Page: The Ultimate Guide for Teachers to Multicultural Literature, written by Dr. Rachel Slaughter, is the quintessential resource for middle school educators. Dr. Slaughter has over thirty years in the field of education as a veteran educator of adolescent learners. Through the skillful combination of her vast teaching experiences and her own qualitative content analysis research of multicultural literature, Dr. Slaughter has expertly created a valuable culturally responsive instructional guide.

Dr. Kara J. Brady
Assistant Professor, Special Education, and School Leadership

Preface

For many people of color, it is emotionally and mentally draining to attend schools where multiculturalism is not acknowledged or celebrated in education and plays no significant part in the curriculum. Students of color often find it difficult to articulate the feelings of loneliness and invisibility they feel in schools where teachers do not fully embrace cultural diversity. These are the students who inspired me to write this book.

While writing the book, I was thinking of the first four chapters as my opportunity to provide statistics on the nation's ever-increasing diversity, the need for multicultural literature in schools, and the obstacles preventing the integration of multicultural literature in schools.

I wrote the remaining four chapters to include the metric school stakeholders can use to think critically about multicultural literature in the effort to choose books free of biased images to complement multicultural education programs. My hope is that the book's short chapters with bullet points answer three important questions:

1. What are the qualities of multicultural literature that adhere to the Common Core States Standards Initiative?
2. How can school stakeholders evaluate literature considered multicultural?
3. What are the reasons school stakeholders reject, ignore, or bypass multicultural literature despite an awareness of the benefits of including the genre in schools?

Including interviews with anti-racist teachers who embrace multiculturalism, the book concludes with an important idea: School stakeholders should create a task force of anti-racist teachers who will use the metric in this book to choose multicultural literature as one component of a multicultural education program that respects and promotes diversity.

In these racially turbulent times, multicultural literature is a perfect academic vehicle to learn about race, racism, and cultural tolerance. Essentially, this book is my prayer for a new normal: Every day, school leaders will show up as anti-racists and do the work of dismantling systemic racism by celebrating diversity using multicultural materials. Maya Angelou wrote: "It is time for parents to teach young people early on that in diversity there is beauty and there is strength."

Multicultural literature is a wonderful way to bridge cultural gaps and become culturally literate while diving into a plethora of worldviews, experiences, and lifestyles. It is my hope that this book inspires educators to do just that.

Acknowledgments

As an avid reader, researcher, and student of multicultural scholars, I have had this book brewing in my soul for many years.

During the process of writing this book, I reached out to several people to whom I would like to extend a warm thank you. My sincere appreciation goes out to the many educators who provided me with recommendations of their favorite multicultural books. Veteran educators like Charlotte Fuller-Jahn, Lisa Rex, Sofia Friedman, Katy Oh, Kathleen Dickerson, Tracie DeLawrence Peterson, and Daphane Davis inspire me with their love of multicultural literature. A special thanks to the scholars who taught me to express myself through writing: Charles Fuller, Dr. Shirley Dixon, and Dr. Jerry Zurek. I would also like to thank Jennie Noakes, my editor.

Finally, I extend my love and appreciation to my mother and reading role model Lillian Fuller, husband Warren T. Slaughter, Jr. and children Chelsea and Sadie Slaughter, and my extended family who cheered me on. As I complete this project, I look forward to turning the page to reveal my next writing adventure.

Chapter 1

Diversity in the Classroom

A Glimpse into the Changing Classroom

Multicultural education was first introduced by scholars like W. E. B. Du Bois and George Washington Williams in the 1900s, who used the concept and mission of multicultural education to challenge the othering of minorities or erasure of their stories. Multicultural educators were determined to promote and celebrate cultural groups to encourage acceptance and understanding. With stories of diverse cultures, these scholars hoped to inspire healthy dialogue among people about race and race relations. In many ways, the early work that the young Black scholars did in the 1900s laid the foundation of Black pride. This is a concept people of color adopted to survive the racial unrest America would experience in the 1950s and 1960s.

In 1954, the ruling in the landmark case of *Brown vs. The Board of Education* ended segregation. At the same time, Black scholars spearheaded the effort to formalize multicultural education and include multicultural materials in the American school curriculum to reflect the minority experience. The integration of the materials in schools was paramount in schools that had been all White and promoting monocultural ideas.

At the time of integration, racial tension was high, as White students shared classrooms with students of color, some for the first time. This racial tension gave birth to meetings that brought students of color and other minority groups together to celebrate cultural diversity. Ultimately, the racial tension and the ensuing demand for cultural representation inspired Black scholars to write and distribute materials that included Black people and other ethnic groups. The materials featuring people of ethnic backgrounds were not well received in schools.

Black educators and scholars designed multicultural education with two important goals in mind: (1) to foster a sense of equity in education and eliminate discrimination and (2) to show children of color images of themselves

1

and others. Although the materials were dedicated to extinguishing negative stereotypical images of Black people and other ethnic groups, there was not an official term for the content. The term "multicultural education" did not appear in print until 1973 in the report titled "No One Model American: A Statement on Multicultural Education," published by the American Association of Colleges of Teacher Education (1973).

MULTICULTURAL EDUCATION: THE PURPOSE

It is estimated that by 2050, ethnic minority children will make up a large part of US public school classrooms, and in some cities, this change has already taken place.

According to the Population Reference Bureau, more than 1 million immigrants who arrive annually are changing the ethnic and racial landscape of the United States. There are over 50 million students enrolled in public schools across the country, and the minority population in these schools is ever increasing. In 2020, the US Census Bureau released the following numbers:

* 13.6 million Hispanic, Latino, and Mexican students
* 2.9 million Asian, Native Hawaiian, and Pacific Islanders students
* 7.7 million Blacks and African American students

The teaching population in US public schools, which is 87 percent White females, is a stark contrast to the ethnically diverse student enrollment. Across the country, many educators are embracing the notion of cultural responsiveness as a means of helping all students reach high standards and celebrate diversity.

Generally, teachers, especially primary school teachers, make the effort to include multicultural literature in their lesson plans. This is true for three reasons. (1) The books are ethnically diverse and highly promoted by publishers. (2) The books are often written by White authors familiar to White teachers. (3) The books are taught in Education courses offered by colleges and universities. Conversely, secondary teachers include fewer multicultural book selections in their lesson plans.

This book details the reasons teachers in secondary education may find it challenging to include multicultural literature, a component of multicultural education, in their lesson plans beginning with the three major obstacles of multicultural education.

MULTICULTURAL EDUCATION:
THREE MAJOR OBSTACLES

The history of multicultural education spans over 100 years; however, the US Department of Education did not make multicultural education mandatory, making it easy for schools to disregard the program. Despite it being promoted as a set of educational strategies that could help students achieve academically, many school stakeholders did not integrate the program into their school curriculum. Why? The answer may exist in the definition of multicultural education. This text reviews the essential elements of multicultural education and how these elements are met with resistance in the school system.

Multicultural education is the "process of comprehensive school reform and basic education for all students that challenges and rejects racism and other forms of discrimination in schools and society, and accepts and affirms pluralism (ethnic, racial, linguistic, religious, economic, and gender)" (Banks and Cherry 2010, 44).

The essential elements in the definition are *comprehensive school reform*, the *rejection of racism and discrimination*, and the *acceptance and affirmation* of one's ethnic, racial, linguistic, religious, and gender identity. These ideas represent the three major issues that affect the successful implementation of multicultural education programs in schools. Although briefly outlined in this chapter, these obstacles are explored in greater detail throughout the book.

- Comprehensive school reform: School reform is conducted by school stakeholders, like school board members and administrators. The changes that school stakeholders make are based in educational research and best practices that help students reach their full academic potential. The result of each school's reform efforts is refined and briefly stated in the school's mission statement, which is politically correct and communicates how the stakeholders of the community value and respect diversity. Conversely, this mission is mooted when there are few mirrors and windows in the curricular material through which the student body can see themselves and others.
- The acceptance and affirmation of one's ethnic, racial, linguistic, religious, and gender identity: This final component of multicultural education starts with the school staffing. Once a diverse faculty is hired, the faculty members must have multicultural materials to teach. Publishing companies produce fewer books by Black, Latinx, or Native American authors than White authors. This lack of books written by authors of color limits the amount of diverse stories available to school stakeholders.

- The rejection of racism and discrimination: In order for multicultural education to thrive, school stakeholders such as board members, faculty members, administrators, and parents must be anti-racist and prepared to discuss and examine the taboo subject of how White privilege and racism are present in the world and negatively impact people of color. Very few discussions about this topic happen in classrooms across the country.

The last point cannot be overstated. The National Association for Multicultural Education (2011), to address multicultural issues in the classroom, set standards for multicultural education. The document states: schools must make every effort to employ "school staff that is culturally competent, and to the greatest extent possible racially, culturally, and linguistically diverse. Staff must be multi-culturally literate and capable of including and embracing families and communities to create an environment that is supportive of multiple perspectives, experiences, and democracy" (p. 1).

This book expands on research which explains how the increase in diversity, along with the inadequate number of culturally literate educators and multicultural books in schools, interferes with the goal of multicultural education becoming a program that helps all students, especially students of color, celebrate diversity. In chapter 2, school reform is defined and promoted as the process school stakeholders need to engage in to successfully incorporate multicultural education in the curriculum.

Chapter 2

Adopting a Multicultural Education Program

Multicultural literature is part of the foundation of multicultural education and has proven to play a major role in the US curriculum and the academic success of all students. Through multicultural materials, students can understand other cultures and perspectives, making it an ideal program to promote diversity.

School stakeholders who hope to adopt a multicultural education program should begin by integrating multicultural literature into the school's curriculum and all parts of the school's culture. Changing the curriculum and school culture are two fundamental steps in school reform, which is a major undertaking and not always well received by faculty members.

What is school reform? School reform, a system of improving schools, involves several components, including resources, best practices, professional development, and school support. In the case of multicultural education, this complex, systemic approach to school improvement requires school stakeholders to adhere to goals meant to acknowledge and respect diversity.

Adhering to the goals of multicultural education will assure the success of a program that moves beyond the memorization of significant facts but also celebrates diversity and provides an appreciation of global awareness in the effort to embrace and honor multiculturalism. What are the ways that school reform efforts and multicultural education interconnect? The goals of school reform and how they dovetail with the goals of multicultural education are briefly described below:

- Serve students using best practices: Many theorists support culturally responsive teaching, which involves teachers being culturally literate, as the most effective pedagogy to close the achievement gap in the rapidly changing demographics of the US education system.

• Garner school support: For a multicultural program to thrive, all stakeholders must agree that the program has value. This is especially important when investing time and money into the program.
• Invest in professional development: Specialized training in multicultural education and its set of strategies is needed since a teacher may lack a background in multicultural education including knowledge of multicultural literature for two major reasons: (1) education majors are not mandated to take courses in race and racism, and (2) few teacher preparation programs feature multicultural literature as a major course of study. Instead education majors are required to study the Western literary canon, which is a collection of works that represents a monocultural experience.
• Provide ample quality resources: School stakeholders who want to create a multicultural education program should begin with choosing and integrating quality multicultural materials. This is difficult to do for two reasons: (1) companies publish fewer books by people of color than their White counterparts, and (2) school stakeholders are wary of their ability to choose bias-free materials since they lack a background in multicultural pedagogy.

The last point is significant. School stakeholders hoping to adopt a multicultural education program often find it difficult to find quality resources to complement the program. Materials are available; however, it is difficult to ascertain the appropriateness of the materials. This is especially true when it comes to multicultural literature. How can school stakeholders determine which books that feature characters of color are suitable for school students when considering factors like stereotypical images that may promote a biased point of view?

A universal rubric to check for the quality of multicultural literature suitable to use in schools could make the process of finding quality multicultural literature easier. Unfortunately, there is none because there is no universal definition for the term "multicultural" or standard for multicultural literature appropriate for schools. The next section describes the elements of quality multicultural literature that complement a multicultural education program.

ELEMENTS OF QUALITY
MULTICULTURAL LITERATURE

Fiction writers use literary devices and techniques to make narratives come alive. Authors are aware that these devices and techniques, commonly referred to as *literary elements*, are essential in the reader's experience.

Essential to the story's foundation, literary elements are plot, setting, and theme. To enhance these literary elements, authors use writing techniques like metaphors, alliteration, and hyperbole.

When writing multicultural fiction, writers must be wary of creating images that have the potential to promote racial stereotypes. The following sections briefly describe ten literary elements that an author of multicultural literature must take into consideration when creating a story that honors multicultural experiences.

Universal Themes

The idea of literary elements including universal themes that relate to the human condition is rooted in the work of the early Greek dramatists, who created epics in all genres, including mystery, romance, and adventure. Racism, freedom, the parent-and-child relationship, the American dream, assimilation, family, courage, friendship, self-discovery, adventure, trust and forgiveness, and peaceful coexistence relationships are the most common universal themes in all literature.

School stakeholders can use the literary element of universal themes to categorize or integrate multicultural literature in the curriculum. For example, a book in the Western canon can be coupled or replaced by a multicultural title sharing the same universal theme. The plot of the two books may be different but share the same theme. Additionally, teachers can use the theme to generate questions or topics for discussions or research papers.

Teachers in upper schools, who are grouped by content areas or departments, use themes to link books to subjects and ideas in the unit lesson plans. Additionally, English department chairs commonly pair with history department chairs to generate a list of books that connects the English and history departments together. This process is sometimes called "teaching across the disciplines." Often teachers will assign writing projects that connect the two disciplines as well. When writing across the disciplines, students can spend time contemplating a certain theme, answer thought questions, or generally thinking critically on paper about what they read.

In the effort to choose multicultural books that affirm personal identity and are biased-free, teachers should critically examine each book selection and the message the book conveys. This critical examination is necessary considering the idea that the standardized curriculum highlights a monocultural experience through materials deemed literary and academic. The questions listed for each section may help a teacher examine each book selection and how the selection aligns with the unit or lesson plan.

Plot

Plot, or the main conflict in the story, is an essential literary device that encompasses the universal theme of the story. Using the plot and the theme, the author conveys aspects of the human condition that are inherent to all people. A writer can convey the plot using many different literary elements that stimulate a reader's imagination, activating their schema and theory of mind. This mental stimulation increases the reader's engagement in the book. Three questions to consider when using plot to evaluate books for a multicultural education program are:

1. Does the plot put characters of color in stereotypical or demeaning situations?
2. How does the plot relate to the theme of the lesson plan or unit?
3. Does the plot describe a set of circumstances or a situation that only people of color can relate to?

Setting

The literary element of setting is especially important when considering multicultural literature since. It is an element of the novel that can highlight an author's implicit bias. When planning a multicultural education program, school stakeholders should recognize that any book labeled as multicultural should feature a setting that is natural in relation to the content of the book and described without stereotypical images. Like the element of plot, there are three questions to consider when using setting to evaluate books for a multicultural education program:

1. Does the author use the setting to put characters of color in stereotypical or demeaning situations?
2. Does the author use words with negative connotations to describe the setting?
3. Is the setting appropriate when considering the plot and characterizations detailed in the book?

Word Choice

Word choice, or how an author uses words, is an expression of the author's point of view. Word choice can influence the reader's perception of the characters as well as affect the tone of the written work.

1. Does the author use words that have negative connotations in association with the characters of color?

2. Can you discern the author's point of view about the characters of color based on his descriptions of the characters?
3. Does the author use profane words? Can you foresee a problem reading the book aloud?

Mood

Mood in literature is the emotions the reader experiences when reading the story. A writer who is gifted in evoking images using words can capture an audience. The mood in a story is a pervasive atmosphere that is present from one page to another. Like the questions in the category of word choice, the questions for mood are centered on how the author makes the reader feel.

1. Does the author use words that conjure up negative feelings in the reader about the characters of color?
2. What emotions do you think the author is trying to evoke in the readers?
3. Do you think the mood will emotionally trigger students of color?

Dialogue

Dialogue, or discourse, which can feature dialect, is the primary literary device that brings a story to life. Discourse or dialogue is the communication between or among characters. Specifically, dialect is a form of a language associated with a specific region or neighborhood. A dialect may seem peculiar when spoken outside of the region where it originated. In a book, dialect can be used as a character trait to emphasize geographical regions, social class, or economic status.

1. Does the author use dialect in a way that accurately represents the character of color's culture, region, lifestyle, or setting of the book?
2. Is the dialect considered stereotypical to the character of color?
3. How will you prepare the students for regional or geographical dialect that is unfamiliar to them?

Imagery

Directly related to the literary element of setting is the element of imagery. How the author describes the setting, characters, and other elements in the story can also reveal the author's implicit bias. Figurative language appeals to the physical senses. The critical questions relating to imagery are like those for mood, word choice, and setting since the author's word choices to describe ideas create images in the reader's mind. In other words, the author's choice of words sparks the reader's imagination.

1. What images in the book seem stereotypical when associated with the characters of color?
2. When considering the images associated with the characters of colors, are they mostly positive or negative?
3. Does each student possess the frame of reference to understand the images the author is trying to convey?

Point of View

In literature, the character's angle of considering things is his point of view. The character's point of view reveals his opinion or feelings regarding a situation. The author uses point of view as a way of narrating the story, which helps the reader stay engaged.

1. Describe the narrator or protagonist of the story? What type of descriptors does the author use to describe the narrator (physical, ethnic, etc.)?
2. What is the narrator's point of view about the characters of color?
3. Can you determine the author's point of view about the characters of color in the book?

Food

Although food is not a literary element, multicultural authors often use food to enhance the cultural aspects of the story. By including culturally relevant food in the novel, the author can establish author credibility or authority on the culture, build a cultural motif, and reveal a conflict. An author who adds foods to the story helps to solidify the cultural background of the characters in the story.

1. Did the author use food to describe the cultural aspects of the characters of color?
2. Did the food choices for the characters of color seem authentic or stereotypical when considering other literary elements like characterization?
3. Did the author use food to enhance each character's background or only the characters of color?

Racial Descriptions

Multicultural literature serves as a vehicle of communicating and illustrating culture and is an integral part of helping students understand the diverse world in which they live. Descriptors that explicitly state each character's race are essential in multicultural literature since these details help the reader know the characters' racial and ethnic backgrounds.

One way to help students appreciate cultural diversity is to present them with a character's physical attributes that are written without bias or stereotype. When an author uses racial descriptors to describe his characters, he must be conscious of words and images that are historically racist. The following questions are meant to imply that certain images are considered inappropriate or racist when associated with characters of color.

1. Does the author create images that compare the character of color to an animal especially primates?
2. Does the author use superlatives to evoke an exaggerated image of the character of color's face or physique?
3. Does the author compare the character of color's skin tone to tar, coal, or other substances that may be considered unpleasant?

Although many authors choose to omit details explicitly describing a character's race and invite the reader to imagine it, including racial descriptors is essential for three reasons:

1. Race and ethnicity encompass biological and sociological factors that can help to establish the story's conflict or theme.
2. Racial descriptors help to categorize the characters as diverse.
3. The descriptions help publishers categorize a book as multicultural, making it easier for librarians, teachers, and parents to locate multicultural materials.

CONCLUSION

Some school stakeholders who are keenly aware of the opportunity to celebrate diversity through multicultural literature want to learn how to incorporate multicultural education into their curriculum. One way to gain some of the benefits of multicultural education is by supplementing the standard curriculum with biased-free multicultural literature. Part of the selection process involves using critical questions to survey each selection. The goal is to find multicultural literature appropriate for school use.

A library of high-quality multicultural literature includes stories about all races, classes, religions, sexualities, abilities, and often-marginalized groups. It should also include a variety of themes, characters, and genres. Ideally, each book's content should mirror the nation's diversity and universality of the human experience. For young readers, especially those living in less diverse communities, these books may be their only experiences with different cultures.

To meet the demands of the general public, companies are publishing more books with diverse characters. School stakeholders need to pursue due diligence in finding multicultural literature that is appropriate for the classroom and aligned with the school's mission. Chapter 3 explores how school stakeholders can pair the elements of quality multicultural literature with critical literacy to evaluate books.

Chapter 3

Critical Literacy and Multicultural Literature

In the effort to reflect ever-increasing diversity of the United States, publishing companies are offering more books featuring culturally diverse characters. Although slight, this increase is one important reason for school stakeholders seeking multicultural literature to understand the qualities of multicultural literature and multiple ways to evaluate the genre for school use.

In the context of this book, quality multicultural literature is defined as literature that "recognizes, accepts, and affirms human differences and similarities related to gender, race, handicap, and class" (Sleeter and Grant 1988, 137). When considering multicultural books for the curriculum, teachers should put their choices through a filter. In other words, it is not safe to assume that all books that include ethnically diverse characters are suitable for the classroom.

Using the reading skill of critical literacy, teachers and students can detect embedded images, ideas, and language that may signal biases or stereotypes. Essentially, critical readers closely examine what they read to discover the author's intended message.

Critical reading is active reading. A critical reader approaches a book or text with an agenda. In the case of a critical reader of multicultural literature, the reader is prepared to survey and "question" the book to find the answers to important questions that may bring to the surface embedded images that are racist or otherwise counterintuitive to the definition of multicultural and a school's mission.

This chapter begins with the utility of critical literacy and continues with an example of critical reading questions. The questions are meant to illustrate critical literacy's main purpose: to help school stakeholders avoid literature that may prove harmful to young minds albeit popular and highly acclaimed.

THE UTILITY OF CRITICAL LITERACY

Paulo Freire (1921–1997), a Brazilian philosopher and influential educator, is considered the father of critical pedagogy, a teaching approach that inspires students to think critically about what they read and challenge authority. Freire helped people think critically about the world by revealing the inequities prevalent in late twentieth century. He encouraged individuals to challenge the system as active and creative thinkers using probing questions. This skill is essential in the work of evaluating multicultural literature, which, in this book, begins with a metric.

The metric is a tool that helps a school stakeholder distinguish quality multicultural literature suitable for the classroom from multicultural literature that may be unfavorable or harmful to a multicultural program. Using the metric included in this book, a school stakeholder may find an author's hidden agenda, reveal unconscious bias, or detect embedded stereotypes.

Critical literacy is a reading tool that promotes reading and is an ideal one for students to learn. Besides reading engagement, critical reading promotes other positive activities. The following ideas are byproducts of reading critically:

- Promote cultural tolerance: Critical literacy skills can spark an enthusiasm for multicultural literature that may lead to a genuine celebration of diversity or cultural tolerance.
- Encourage dialogue: A teacher who promotes critical literacy creates a space for the teacher and student to discuss the current racial climate as well as contest the ideology of cultural superiority and monoculturalism present in many schools.
- Detect systemic racism: Students can use critical literacy to recognize systemic inequities and engage in conversations about race relations with teachers who help unpack the complexities of race and culture.
- Compare multiple sources: Teachers can teach their students to question everything they read while using primary and secondary sources or documents to corroborate cultural information, events, or settings.

The next section examines how critical literacy helps a reader when evaluating books involving protagonists of color. This examination encourages readers to use multiple sources to help understand the author's background and qualifications for writing the story of their choice.

To be included in a multicultural education program, any author who depicts members of an Indigenous, marginalized, or ethnic group must refrain from dehumanizing the characters with biased or stereotypical information or point of view. Through research of an author's background and authority on the subject, readers can determine an author's point of view and evaluate the message he is sending in his story.

THINKING CRITICALLY ABOUT
AUTHORS' AUTHORITY

Euripides said, "Question everything. Learn something. Answer nothing." This is a profound mantra and the fundamental premise of critical literacy. Before selecting a book that includes people of color, a reader should first critically examine the author's background. When reviewing information regarding the author's biographical background, professional associations, formal, and informal education, a critical reader can determine the author's authority on a subject.

Critical literacy is especially useful when reading books written by authors who write about experiences, identities, or cultures outside of their own reality or identity. Often authors, who write about stories outside of their cultural background, meet skepticism and accusations of misrepresentation, racism, or cultural appropriation. The accusations stem from the idea that authors in dominant cultural groups who chose to write about non-dominant cultural groups lack the proper background, research, or authority to portray the cultural characteristics associated with the non-dominant cultural groups.

Although it is sometimes difficult to ascertain a person's intent, a reader can use critical literacy to gather information to make an informed decision.

In this section, the novel *The Cay* (New York: Yearling, 2002) by Theodore Taylor, is used to show how critical questions may help use textual evidence to learn the author's background and determine how his background may inform his point of view on race. First published in 1969, the novel has been republished many times.

- Cultural connection: Do the author and the protagonist share the same ethnic background? Theodore Taylor, a White native of North Carolina, creates two protagonists. One protagonist, Phillip, is an adolescent White boy and the other is Timothy, an old West Indian man.
- Authority: How did the author obtain information about the Indigenous people or culture portrayed in the book? Taylor, a former naval office, was a world traveler. In many interviews, Taylor explains that Phillip, the White character, represents a childhood friend whose parents taught him to despise Black people.
- Author's biography: Does the author's biographical background connect to the Indigenous people or culture portrayed in the book? In his autobiography, Taylor recounts growing up in North Carolina and being terrified

of white-robed Klansmen with torches who stormed past his house. The autobiography also details Taylor's friendly encounters with the people of the Caribbean.

AUTHOR'S WORD CHOICE AND PEOPLE OF COLOR

When evaluating an author's book, the reader should carefully examine the author's choice of words to describe the characters of color. In this section, Taylor's word choice in *The Cay* is examined.

Word choice is essential when telling stories involving characters of color since the denotation of certain words can evoke racist images when associated with characters of color and their physical features. The depictions of people of color must be closely examined for the sake of providing students with images that respect people of color and the nuances of their experiences.

- Word choice: What words, ideas, or images in the book help you determine the author's feelings about the culture depicted? In the novel, Taylor describes Timothy and his physical features: "A huge, very old Negro. He was ugly. His nose was flat, and his face was broad" (Taylor 1969, 28). The word "ugly" is a negative one when associated with a person's looks. The word "broad" has a negative connotation when associated with a black person's physical features. For example, historically, the word "broad" was used to describe a Black person's nose in contrast to a European person's nose, which is often described as thin and viewed as elegant. In American culture, thin is considered the ideal when associated with facial features or physicality.
- Literary elements: What literary elements does the author use to conjure up images in the reader's mind? Taylor uses a metaphor to describe the contrast of Timothy's gums to his teeth: "His teeth made an alabaster trench in his mouth, and his pink-purple lips peeled back over them like the meat of a conch shell" (Taylor 1969, 28). Again, the use of the word "purple" is one that is considered derogatory to Black people because it is linked to anti-Black imagery and language meant to demean people with dark skin.

Using secondary sources, the reader will find important details about the book. For example, research shows that Taylor's book was not well received in the African American community. The plot and the author's word choices or images were cited as racist.

Despite the criticism, in 1974, the novel was made into a motion picture starring James Earl Jones as Timothy. The movie, which has the same title as the book, tells the story of an unusual friendship between a White boy and an

African slave. In the movie and book, Phillip shows a disdain for Timothy, which is evident in his description of the man as "black and ugly" or "big Negro" (Taylor 1969, 33). The author writes, "He smiled at me, his face becoming less terrifying" (Taylor 1969, 28).

In the book, readers will find that much of Phillip's feelings about Black or African people are directly related to his parents' sentiments and warnings. His mother was adamant that Phillip should not associate with Black or African people because she didn't like them. His mother told him, "They are not the same as you. They are different and live differently" (Taylor, 1969, 40). Before their friendship is solidified, Phillip thinks of Timothy as "just a stupid old black man" (Taylor 1969, 59).

The quotes from the book are significant since they may indicate the author's bias toward Indigenous people. In the instance of *The Cay*, the inclusion of biased images is in direct opposition to the framework of multicultural education. Additionally, the language and overall messages in the novel do not support the idea of celebrating culture, particularly the African culture. Therefore, this book has no place in a multicultural education program.

MULTICULTURAL LITERATURE AND THE N-WORD

Vernacular, slang, or language pattern that is particular or peculiar to a specific region or social group in a book is always a hotbed topic in schools. The language pattern also represents another item that school stakeholders can use to evaluate a multicultural book.

A writer may use informal speech like slang to provide readers with an accurate characterization of protagonists of color, time period, neighborhood surroundings, or milieu. To communicate authenticity, the pattern of speaking must be genuine for the character depicted. This is the case in historical fiction and the use of the n-word. When offering a slice of history in a novel, the author is somewhat compelled to use the language of that time period.

Although the n-word is used in a historical context in some books, teachers should keep in mind that the word has always had a negative connotation when White people use it in reference to Black, African American, or African people. In other words, when teachers come across this word in historical fiction, the word should be treated as one that is insulting, degrading, and dehumanizing.

The n-word has a complicated history but is widely used in pop culture. School stakeholders who choose to select multicultural literature that includes the n-word must explore the history and nuances of the word with students and other school stakeholders. This exploration helps the stakeholders, especially teachers and students, to understand the word's complexities and develop a position on the word's use in the school community. It is wise to consult an expert on this topic. School stakeholders may start with researchers like Neal A. Lester, professor of English and founding director of Project Humanities at Arizona State University.

CONCLUSION

Critical questions help a reader pay close attention to possible racist images, messages, and language that can seep into the reader's schema, and shape cognition, emotion, motivation, and behavior. Keep in mind, however, an author who incorporates biased or stereotypical images in his work may do so without malice. He may be unaware of the negative connotations of his word choices.

In order to secure literature that respects people's cultures and identities, school stakeholders must be committed to doing the work that will uncover biased or stereotypical images. This work includes reading the novel critically and researching the author's background to determine his authority on the subject and possibly his intentions for writing the novel.

Reading critically is worth the effort since the activity helps school stakeholders reject books that may promote harmful images. Using probing and critical questions, school stakeholders can examine their literary choices to determine if the selections fit the school's needs.

The questions in this chapter represent a fragment of the research school stakeholders should undertake when selecting quality multicultural literature because a body of well-researched multicultural literature is the foundation of a successful multicultural education program. In chapter 4, the QUILT metric, an additional critical literacy tool, is used to examine literature.

Chapter 4

Generating a List of Multicultural Books

Teachers find it a daunting task to locate and include multicultural books in the curriculum, allowing "colorblind" ideology to prevail in most American classrooms. Interested in choosing multicultural literature appropriate for schools, school stakeholders have expressed the need for a handy critical reading resource that helps them identify multicultural books which reflect our diverse world.

To generate an initial list of multicultural books, teachers can use online resources and databases such as Diverse Book Finder and the Cooperative Children's Book Center. These databases provide necessary information about the book's genre, plot, and character descriptions. More research is needed, however, when choosing which books on the list are appropriate, or otherwise worthy for school use. How can a school stakeholder distinguish between a book that includes characters of color from a book oppositional to the school's curriculum or diversity mission?

A quick and easy way to assess the quality of a particular book is to use the QUILT metric. The acronym QUILT stands for the Quality of writing, Universal theme, Imaginative plot, Lesson plan, and Talking points. The points in the metric help teachers evaluate and select multicultural books that align with the standard curriculum.

In the next section, there is a list of ideas and questions that correspond with the metric and prompt school stakeholders to think critically about important aspects of each book.

THE QUILT METRIC

Quality of Writing

The quality of writing, which includes the literary elements, is what makes a good book stand out. When trying to determine the quality of writing in multicultural literature, there are a few literary concepts to consider.

- Writing style: Style describes the ways that the author uses words, sentence structure, figurative language, and sentence arrangement to convey his message. The novel's content should be easily recognized and understood by members of the culture portrayed. Similarly, readers outside of the culture should be able to understand the content as well.
- Word choice: When creating images using figurative language like similes and metaphors to describe the physical characteristics of people of color, the author should choose words that depict the culture with respect. He should always be knowledgeable and conscious of his biases, biographical background, historically racist-based language, and how these elements may affect his outlook or the reader's perception about the story he is sharing.
- Imagery and setting: The primary setting is natural in relation to the content of the book and described without using stereotypes. Additionally, the setting should be universal instead of "typical" to the culture in a stereotypical way.
- Point of view: A character's point of view may reveal the author's bias on an idea and should be carefully considered when school stakeholders are choosing books for a multicultural education program.

Universal Theme

A universal theme in literature is a general lesson that readers can learn from the story, regardless of their ethnic background, religious belief, or sexual orientation. It conveys aspects of the human condition that are inherent to all people. The most popular multicultural books are written by authors who are gifted in presenting human behavior and multiple dimensions of a culture objectively and without biased images.

Imaginative Plot

The author's style and quality of writing makes the plot intriguing and engaging so that the reader is compelled to consider the universal theme or lesson the theme illustrates.

Lesson Plans

School stakeholders should align their selections to the themes in their curriculum. Teachers should use the selected books to illustrate those themes when writing lesson plans.

Talking Points for Class Discussions

In general, talking points are topics extrapolated from a presentation that the speaker can use to generate a lively discussion. Talking points are useful to teachers as well. When writing lesson plans, a teacher should consider what topics in the multicultural book would be ideal to highlight in a discussion. Including the talking points in the lesson plans helps a teacher keep the lesson focused on a learning goal since class discussions can become an arena for student opinions. With this idea in mind, teachers should take precautions and set guidelines for class discussions. The following are a few ideas and questions to consider before initiating a class discussion:

- Cultural sensitivity: When creating talking points, a teacher must be keenly aware of the student audience and sensitive to controversial topics that may offend or hurt anyone's feelings. Does the book include ideas, terms, and images that are culturally insensitive and controversial? Is the teacher equipped with the necessary background information to answer any questions regarding the identified culture? Should the teacher consult an expert on the topic before starting the lesson? Does the plot indirectly identify a student in class?
- Racial sensitivity: Victims of racism can experience triggers when reading or discussing certain ideas in books. Sometimes, just reading or recounting racially charged incidents can ignite feelings of anxiety in victims. Teachers must take care to exhibit racial sensitivity when engaging in discussions with students. Does the book include racially charged incidents? Did the teacher establish a safe space to recount incidents of racism?
- Background knowledge: In order for students to fully engage in a lesson, they must have some background knowledge of the subject. Essential to comprehension, background knowledge or frame of reference is the key to readiness or the mental ability for a student to accept the idea presented. It is different from the cognitive ability to understand the material. Does each student possess a background or familiarity with the subject? If so, how was the knowledge acquired and assessed?
- Teacher bias: Before presenting books that depict characters of color to students, a teacher should be keenly aware of his biases. How does the teacher connect to the subject? Does the teacher have any biases regarding the characters depicted?

CONCLUSION

In classrooms, multicultural literature can be a powerful catalyst for conversations about race and other identities. Aware of their own limitations in assessing the quality of multicultural books, some teachers may not trust themselves to find the appropriate books to engage students. The QUILT metric is a tool that will help teachers with the process of selecting books. School stakeholders serve their school communities well when they prioritize literature and conversations about cultural diversity. When teachers approach these stories with sensitivity, it helps to create safe spaces for students to feel comfortable with talking about issues of race.

The manner in which students come to perceive their social world depends upon the carefully selected resources available to them. Chapter 5 includes information on how to create a task force of school stakeholders who are willing to devote their time to doing the much needed research of choosing multicultural literature that aligns with school standards.

Chapter 5

Creating a Task Force

A school task force dedicated to finding multicultural literature that celebrates diversity can help school stakeholders create an inclusive curriculum. This chapter examines the idea of forming a task force charged with creating a multicultural, anti-racist book list that will provide students with literary experiences dealing with diverse perspectives and lifestyles.

Which school stakeholder should consider becoming a member of the task force? Every member of the task force must welcome the inclusion of multicultural literature as the first step in the effort to recognizing diversity. Furthermore, each member must keep in mind the ultimate goal of the task force: to help the community understand race and the issues of racism while celebrating cultural differences in order to eliminate misunderstandings and create a sense of community in schools.

As part of his own personal development, each member is willing to examine his biases to determine how his feelings, actions, and words affect a relationship with each student. Furthermore, the task force member is prepared to challenge White privilege and the systemic oppression of racial minorities at every turn.

Task force members will be considered allies who use a critical lens on the education system to examine White privilege while revealing systemic racism. This is an important work since institutional racism is an academic disease that affects students of color across the nation. What can each school stakeholder do to hone his skills as a member of the task force?

THE PROFESSIONAL DEVELOPMENT
OF A TASK FORCE MEMBER

A task force member is a role model of the school's mission or platform regarding diversity and multicultural education. Each member of the task force must be an anti-racist who actively denounces racism and monoculturalism and promotes cultural diversity. How does this look daily?

- Participate in ongoing professional development: Since information about multicultural education is constantly evolving, each member of the task force should research and participate in professional development that provides comprehensive cultural literacy workshops and diversity training to increase cultural literacy and cultural intelligence.
- Commit to challenging racism: Since multicultural literature can instigate discussions about race and racism, each member must formally learn effective strategies to recognize and discuss White fragility, White backlash, and other instances of racism.
- Become an expert in critical literacy: Critical literacy is a reading skill that helps readers unpack racial stereotypes present in our society. Each stakeholder should become competent in this reading strategy to question negative cultural images in the Western canon, news, and pop culture.

TASK FORCE RESPONSIBILITIES

Although institutional racism is at the foundation of the US school system, it may be difficult to recognize since it is systemic and ubiquitous. Along with many other responsibilities, as anti-racists, task force members would be charged with recognizing, pinpointing, and dismantling systemic racism that prevent the opportunity for students and school stakeholders to maintain a multicultural program.

Here are seven ways the task force can address institutional racism while creating and maintaining a multicultural education program centered on multicultural literature.

1. Decide on best practices: The task force can help choose the best practices that teachers will use to highlight multicultural literature.
2. Review, revise, and implement school policies: The task force can review school policies that may impede inclusion of a multicultural education program. Additionally, the task force can help influence naysayers about the benefits of multicultural education while addressing institutionalized racism and monoculturalism.

3. Design a course in race relations: The course can help students understand the constructs of racism and the destruction racism (including systemic racism) has caused in our society.

4. Celebrate cultural diversity: The task force can provide students with information about underrepresented cultures through stories of everyday people. It can assist faculty members in finding ways to resist the urge to regard multicultural literature as episodic or supplementary to their curriculum.

5. Examine historical accounts using critical literacy: Task force members can teach school stakeholders and students how to use critical literacy to question historical accounts especially those found in textbooks. Critical literacy helps readers detect one-dimensional stories of heroification that use partial or inaccurate information to glorify individuals in our history.

6. Challenge colorblindness: Task force members can help school stakeholders challenge instances of colorblindness, which along with White privilege, poses incredible challenges for students of color, including the necessity of seeing themselves in the curriculum.

7. Become good listeners: Task force members can identify themselves as the "listeners" in the community by providing spaces for students of color to detail their experiences with racism.

CONCLUSION

School stakeholders in US schools have the power to change the curriculum to include multicultural literature. The best way to accomplish this mission is to create a task force dedicated to integrating the genre into the curriculum. Each member of the task force, as an anti-racist ally, must actively reject White privilege and White supremacy and explain how these forms of racism can adversely affect students.

The task force work is vital since the diverse student body and their allies are demanding multicultural literature that respectfully depicts people of color with voices that describe their unique positions in this world. It is important to point out that multicultural literature is available, but it just isn't prevalent in schools, creating a sense of inequality and oppression in the US curriculum.

Designed to cast a critical eye on the curriculum and the daily messages the White teachers are sending through their speech, actions, and literary choices, the task force will do some heavy lifting. Chapter 6 examines the summer reading list, an important project for the task force and the first step to spearheading a culturally responsive effort of integrating the school's curriculum with multicultural literature.

Chapter 6

The Multicultural Summer Reading List

A multicultural education program presents opportunities for educating people about racism which poses incredible challenges for people of diverse backgrounds. Unfortunately, the US Department of Education does not require or recommend a multicultural education program. How can school stakeholders incorporate multicultural literature in the standard curriculum that is difficult to amend? A fluid curricular entity that may change each year, a summer reading list is the best vehicle to provide required and optional reading selections that celebrate diversity and align with the school's mission.

THE FUNCTIONS OF A MULTICULTURAL SUMMER READING LIST

Multicultural literature has many proven benefits, including helping students of color achieve academically. Along with the benefits, a multicultural summer reading list offers school stakeholders opportunities to accomplish important tasks. For example, here is a list of projects that cohere with a multicultural, comprehensive summer reading list.

- Provide supplementary materials and resources: Since the curriculum is not easily amended, school stakeholders can create an addendum to the curriculum using the summer reading program as the catalyst.
- Create a resource center: The multicultural summer reading books and associated materials can be integrated into the library or resource center for use during the school year.
- Share resources: A multicultural education program can be difficult to create and sustain. Sharing the multicultural reading list with other schools

can help school stakeholders who are in search of quality multicultural resources.

- Encourage workplace diversity: Promoting a multicultural summer reading list can help people of color feel valued.
- Prepare future graduates: A review of the top ten private schools in the United States reveals that school mission statements are focused on helping students prepare future professionals for an increasingly diverse world.
- Mold adolescent minds: Offering a multicultural summer reading list is a concerted effort to integrate multicultural materials into the curriculum. This is important since, beginning in eighth grade, three important developments occur: (1) eighth grade marks the senior year of middle school for the private school sector, (2) the topics gleaned from the eighth grade summer reading materials are the first ideas discussed in ninth grade, (3) adolescents reach puberty in the eighth grade and are keenly aware of their cultural similarities, differences, social identity, and biases.
- Create talking walls: The multicultural summer reading books provide ideas for anti-racist messaging that school stakeholders can promote on posters displayed on school walls and conveyed in school media.
- Encourage open dialogue: The multicultural summer reading literature includes subjects that can spark dialogue about multicultural issues.

SELECTING MULTICULTURAL LITERATURE AND OTHER POINTS TO EXPLORE

To begin selecting books, the task force should set up criteria that align with the curriculum. The following list provides information that the task force members can use as a guide to create a list of standards designed with the school's curriculum in mind. This list of standards can be shared with faculty members and other school stakeholders as an indication of criteria that define the summer reading list for the school.

Example criteria for a summer reading list could be as follows:

- Fiction books: Nonfiction books and biographies are excluded since these two genres do not present an opportunity for teachers to use literary universal themes as topics for class discussions.
- Publishing: Books should be published by major publishing companies. This criterion excludes vantage publishers.
- Hard copies: The books should be distributed in hard copy, which excludes electronic books.
- Language: Books should be printed in English, excluding books written in foreign languages.

- Characters: To be considered in the review, the books on the list must include a protagonist who is a person of color or of a non-dominant racial group, which excludes books with characters of color but without a protagonist of color.
- Author: To reduce instances of possible bias or stereotypes, the author of each book should have firsthand knowledge of the protagonist of color's culture.

Multicultural literary selections offer a cornucopia of perspectives stemming from multicultural, cross-cultural, and intercultural experiences. Briefly defined in this section, these perspectives may prompt the task force to address or explore the following ideas:

- Multicultural aspects: What cultures are represented in the novel? Do people of different cultures interact with each other in the book? How is each culture represented?
- Diversity of themes: What themes are most prevalent in the summer reading selections? What central idea does the body of multicultural literature communicate? Do all of the books represent one theme?
- Mental health: Does the body of literature take into consideration students' mental health? Does the theme of racial violence and racial tension come up often in the list? Do the images in the books increase students' feelings of trauma? How will the themes in the selections make the students feel?
- Student empowerment: Do the themes promote student empowerment and positive racial engagement and harmony?
- Critical literacy: What critical reading questions will help the reader explore the book's ideas or uncover the hidden messages?
- Author's authority: Can a person who is not of a particular culture or identity accurately portray that culture in writing? In what ways does the author of the book have firsthand knowledge of the culture depicted in the book?

EVALUATING MULTICULTURAL LITERATURE
FOR THE SUMMER READING LIST

A task force charged with the responsibility of finding quality multicultural will need to dedicate at least four weeks to the project of evaluating the list of potential summer reading choices. How can the task force, focused on honoring diversity, evaluate and offer multicultural literature? The project involves many steps, but few materials.

The first step is selecting a preliminary list of books. This begins with gathering additional information about each book on the proposed multicultural summer reading list. Task force members can find book details on websites like Bookrags.com, Amazon.com, and Publishers Weekly. These sites are especially helpful to determine each book's theme, page count, publishing date, and synopsis.

The second step is for each task force member to choose a reading partner. The partners will each read the same book. The final step is to gather and distribute the necessary materials needed for the reading project: the selected books, notebooks, pencils, sticky notes, the QUILT metric and critical questions in chapter 4 (see appendix B: Table B.1).

THE QUILT METRIC AND READER'S JOURNAL

Each book should be read by two readers who mark the book with abbreviations relating to the items in the metric. Easy or common abbreviations may include writing style (WS), word choice (WC), and point of view (POV). The readers can distinguish areas in the book relating to the metric with colored highlighters. The reader may mark meaningful units of information like words, phrases, sentences, and objects that relate to each category.

As part of the reading process, each reader can keep a "reader's journal" to jot down ideas, thoughts, or "aha" moments about the books as he reads. For example, the notes in the journal may reflect the reader's thoughts or serve as a place to write details about the author's background. Once the partners have read each book, they should compare notes. In other words, the readers should use their notes to determine, based on the metric, if the book is suitable for a summer reading choice for the multicultural summer reading list.

CONCLUSION

Task force members, which may include parents and other school stakeholders, should be mindful that multicultural education and its corresponding literature are focused on people of color whose identities, contributions, and histories "have been omitted, distorted, and undervalued in society and school curriculum" (Bishop 1997, 3). With this idea in mind, the task force can create a master list of quality multicultural books, informed by a peer-reviewed metric and vetted by anti-racist teachers, administrators, and librarians well versed in quality multicultural literature.

The work in finding and selecting the books can be an overwhelming task. For this reason, the work is best left to task force members who can dedicate the time needed to engage in the evaluation process with fidelity.

Essentially, the summer reading list is the source of books that will help children see themselves and others while vicariously experiencing situations that are outside of their purview. Not all members of the faculty will welcome this intense focus on multicultural literature. Chapter 7 explores possible obstacles that the task force may encounter when trying to integrate multicultural literature into the curriculum.

Chapter 7

The Task Force Meets
Resistance and Bias

The task force that is dedicated to finding, securing, and implementing multi-cultural literature in the school's curriculum may encounter resistance rooted in colorblind ideology. For example, some faculty members may contend that they "don't see color," a need to highlight racism, or celebrate culture in the curriculum. Other faculty members may balk at the summer reading list in favor of selections from the Western canon, the body of literature of which they may be most familiar.

In general, task force members may experience a faculty member's distaste for the information about multicultural literature through coded racist statements, refusal to examine his biases, or issues of systemic racism that maintain the status quo. Through resistance and White backlash, a faculty member may thwart the multicultural summer reading list.

To combat issues of colorblindness, institutional, and individual racism, school stakeholders must do a critical race analysis of the school. Rooted in Critical Race Theory, this analysis makes race the center of an examination. A critical race analysis may begin with an introspective examination of the school's curriculum and continue with an exploration of each faculty member's biases through the same lens. In many cases, biases stem from a lack of experience with diversity in the teacher's neighborhood, friendship circle, or college preparatory studies.

THE TASK FORCE AND TEACHERS

As part of critical race analysis, a quick survey of the faculty may reveal something very interesting: few teachers studied multicultural education in college. Many colleges or universities do not offer comprehensive, mandatory multicultural programs in the education department for fledgling teachers. These courses include content integration, the knowledge construction process, prejudice reduction, equity pedagogy (Banks 1995a), and courses on race, diversity, and inclusion.

Preservice teachers are not required to take courses on race, race relations, racism, and the social constructs that may support institutional racism. Studies show, even when White students are enrolled in courses surveying multicultural literature, they tend to show resistance to the information. They express their irritation and prejudice through seemingly innocent jokes, snide remarks, or strategic eye contact with other White people in the room. These actions establish a "bond" among the White people who have distaste for the course.

The "bonding" behavior may be off-putting to students of color and may even deter the facilitator from teaching the course effectively. This last point is significant since the preservice teachers eventually land fulltime jobs as faculty members of established academic institutions across the country and may need to rely on information they missed in class.

RESISTANCE AND THE WESTERN CANON

A teacher's lack of background in multicultural education makes integrating multicultural materials into an educational system that supports the Western canon challenging. This challenge may dismay a teacher prompting him to seek materials that are more familiar to him. For example, teachers are often thrilled to teach the Western canon they were taught to love during their schooling. This is the primary body of literature studied in Education courses in most universities. However, educators must keep in mind that the canon is deliberately put together with the purpose of excluding certain literary works, creating an abbreviated body of literature and limited view of the world (Bates 2013, 1).

For quality multicultural literature to become an integral part of the school system, school administrators and teachers must be willing to release the notion that the canon is the most important body of work. The idea cannot be overstated: students will benefit from a multicultural curriculum.

TALKING ABOUT RACE IN THE CLASSROOM

Multicultural literature presents opportunities to discuss race in the classroom. The literature, however, must be bias free since materials that include biased images negatively skew a student's perceptions of a specific culture and ultimately affect students of color and their performance in school.

Despite the use of carefully selected multicultural literature, students may show resistance to participating in discussions about race and racism because these discussions make them feel uncomfortable. It is important to note that students of color are conditioned by the US curriculum, White female educators, and stakeholders to ignore race and sometimes culture. This is why a student of color may have a difficult time articulating microaggressions and cultural insensitivity he has endured. Over time, perhaps years after he has left the institution, these feelings will surface, giving the student an opportunity to address his feelings of racial trauma.

A White student may also show disdain for talking about race in the classroom. This feeling may stem from three issues:

1. It is difficult for a White student to identify, address, and unlearn White privilege.
2. A White student is wary of being called out as a racist.
3. A White student may experience the feeling of "White fatigue" or the feeling that the subject of race is one that is exhausting to discuss since "we always talk about it and it the discussion gets us nowhere."

Many White students understand racism exists but "are not yet situated to fully understand the complexity of racism and how it functions as an institutional and systemic phenomenon" (Flynn, 2015, 115). Talking about race is sure to trigger an emotional response from all participants involved. In leading conversations about various forms of racism, including individual and systemic, teachers will encounter typical reactions from White students and students of color.

In general, most students of color are cautious when discussing race matters but secretly maintain hope that a discussion about race will lead to racial harmony and cultural tolerance. Specifically, students of color yearn for compassion and acknowledgment of racism and feelings of racial stress or trauma while hoping that their White peers and White teachers act as allies and stand up when racism is in motion. Young people call this being "woke."

HOW TO BE A "WOKE" TEACHER

Being "woke," or acknowledging that racism exists in our present-day society, may be difficult for a White teacher to achieve. In some cases, a teacher may feel anger, fear, or guilt when acknowledging how racism or White privilege presents in schools or in society. Here are four steps a teacher can follow to foster healthy race discussions in the classroom while acknowledging racism:

1. Seek out professional development including resources that put you in touch with experts in the field of talking about race with students: Teachers should become well versed in talking about race, racism, and White privilege and how these ideas present in our society.
2. Examine personal biases: Since it is common to make assumptions about people based on race, the teacher should examine his own personal biases (see appendix B: textbox 1).
3. Create a safe space: Offer students a place to share their experiences with racism. Since each person is speaking from the "I" perspective, establish rules or boundaries that will protect students from accusatory language or other verbally violent responses.
4. Encourage reading and writing: A teacher can encourage a thoughtful dialogue by adding reading and writing activities into the lesson plan. Students can read relevant selections, write responses, and use their written responses as part of the discussion. These activities encourage deep reflection and eliminate the opportunity for quick quips or one liners that could diminish another person's experiences.

CONCLUSION

Despite the benefits of incorporating multicultural literature in the curriculum, school stakeholders including task force members may meet resistance to the idea of a multicultural summer reading list or amending the standard curriculum to reflect a multicultural program. For any part of a multicultural education program to thrive in a school, the faculty members must be anti-racist professionals who are prepared to confront and discuss racism with members of the school community. These conversations are vital to the well-being of any student body. In chapter 8, ideas and questions that encourage school stakeholders in normalizing multiculturalism while subscribing to a culturally responsive teaching pedagogy are detailed.

Chapter 8

How to Normalize Multiculturalism

The ultimate goal of multicultural literature is to promote respect for other people through intercultural understanding, and a sense of belonging. To this end, the inclusion of quality multicultural literature in the school curriculum can lead to the celebration of diversity and cultural norms, helping students to appreciate each other on a deeper level.

The goal of this book is to provide school stakeholders with tools, including a list of standards that identify the qualities and sources of multicultural literature. However, the information in this book will not dismantle systemic racism. To combat this form of racism, school stakeholders must examine every part of the academic institution with "ally eyes" while working to normalize multiculturalism.

What three moves should school stakeholders make with ally eyes:

1. Focused on the standard curriculum, school stakeholders should remove materials and literature that underscore a monocultural point of view.
2. Next, they must create and execute a plan of school reform centered on multiculturalism.
3. Finally, they should hire and train teachers who identify as anti-racist and are willing to engage in professional development that provides best practices for all students, but especially students of color who have been marginalized and ignored in a standard curriculum that was not designed with them in mind.

THE STANDARD CURRICULUM

The US curriculum needs an upgrade. Designed, in the 1700s, the first standard curriculum was invented to teach White children how to run farms more effectively. At the same time, enslaved Black people were trying to teach their children to read and write in secret, despite threats to their lives. In the 1900s, in the face of staunch opposition, Black scholars promoted multicultural education in schools. Designed to celebrate other cultures and reflect diverse experiences, multicultural education became the symbol of Black resistance and the Civil Rights Movement in the 1960s.

Consider the Black literary societies of the nineteenth century. Members of these groups met to socialize and debate issues of politics and education. These groups of free Black people in antebellum north were formed in cities like Philadelphia, Boston, Chicago, and Washington, D.C. Their collective mission was to promote themselves as academicians and use education to assert themselves in political and literary circles. These scholars encouraged Black artists, writers, and orators who would later dominate the Harlem Renaissance.

A prominent educator and member of a Black literary society was William Edward Burghardt Du Bois. Known as W. E. B. Du Bois (1868–1963), he was a scholar, civil rights activist, and founder of the National Association for the Advancement of Colored People (NAACP). He vehemently opposed racism and fought for equal rights for Black people. From 1884 to 1888, as a college student at Fisk University, he spent his summers teaching in rural Black schools in Nashville, Tennessee. After becoming the first Black person to receive a doctorate from Harvard University, Du Bois became a professor and prolific writer of academic articles and textbooks and novels.

Over the years, unable to fight institutional and individual racism, multicultural education scholars and supporters watched multicultural education be reduced to extraneous elements of multicultural education like Black history facts and a few books in schools. Despite the promise of measurable gains in student performance, the US Department of Education did not mandate schools to integrate multicultural education into the standard curriculum. Furthermore, since there is no national curriculum, each state can dictate its own curriculum with little guidance from the US Department of Education making it easier for school stakeholders to ignore multicultural education.

In a concerted effort to normalize multiculturalism, a task force dedicated to finding quality multicultural literature can integrate appropriated selections into the curriculum, starting with the summer reading list. This list, which is usually independent of the standard curriculum, has the capacity to inform a school's curriculum and reflect any diversity initiatives. The multicultural summer reading list, when advertised and promoted, will attract students and faculty of color who value multiculturalism.

SCHOOL REFORM

Multicultural education may be doomed to a state of limbo because it relies on school reform in order to thrive. School reform is difficult to execute with fidelity since it encompasses several major components, including substantial resources, best practices, professional development, measurable goals, and stakeholders' (especially teachers') support. Normally, major decisions regarding school reform are made by the board of education. These decisions begin with committee meetings that may inform board policies. In general, it is a lot of red tape.

School reform is necessary in order to challenge the systemic obstacles that impede the adoption of a curriculum that includes literature detailing the struggles of Indigenous people or people of color and celebrates the cultural contributions of racialized people globally and nationally. If your school stakeholders are prepared to begin the work of school reform, the following questions and ideas may be good place to start:

Substantial resources: What resources can you read or garner that will help the school stakeholders understand multicultural education, its components, and benefits? Multicultural materials are not prolific, but they are available. In order to access these materials, school stakeholders should subscribe to digital resources like Readbrightly.com and Thebrownbookshelf.com that feature curated sources of multicultural materials including multicultural literature. Other resources that help students understand and celebrate our diverse world include Teachingforchange.org, Rethinkingschools.org, Tolerance.org, and Edchange.org. Additionally, to access research articles, school stakeholders may subscribe to peer-reviewed, scholarly journals like *The International Journal of Multicultural Education, American Journal of Education*, and *Education and Urban Society Journal*. Professional development opportunities are available at local and national conferences featuring multicultural education scholars.

Best practices: In what ways will the faculty and other school stakeholders use best practices in education to highlight multicultural education? Teachers who expect to teach in schools with students of different cultures need to subscribe to best practices for teaching diverse students. Additionally, to help understand the minds of young people, teachers should be well versed in child psychology. The study of a child's conscious and subconscious mind and the impact of social constructs on their psyche helps inform teaching practices.

Measurable goals: What goals will school stakeholders set to measure the effectiveness of the multicultural education program? School stakeholders should strive to create a program that underscores educational equity and celebrates diversity. Additionally, school stakeholders need to form a community of adults and mentors who are anti-racist, compassionate, and prepared to value a vocation of selfless service.

Feedback: How will you collect feedback about the multicultural education program? Feedback or constructive criticism is essential to the improvement of any program. School stakeholders, especially school administrators, should take the time to survey the students with the hope of receiving candid responses. This raw data will help school stakeholders make notable changes to improve the program. Keep in mind that inviting students to provide informal feedback through candid or impromptu discussions is just as important as collecting data from formal surveys. A very quick and easy feedback activity is the exit ticket. This tool allows a teacher to assess how students are feeling, at the end of class, through a very short hardcopy or online survey.

Stakeholders' support: Who are the school stakeholders willing to support multicultural education? In general, school institutions are managed by school boards or boards of trustees. A board's prime responsibility is to ensure student success through the implementation of effective academic resources. It is the entity that monitors how school stakeholders are meeting the school's objectives or school mission.

Professional development: In what ways can you help faculty members prepare to teach courses that encompass multicultural education? School stakeholders must make hiring anti-racist teachers a priority. Professional development will provide ongoing learning opportunities to sharpen the skills needed to support a successful multicultural program. These skills include communication, relationship building, and behavior management.

School stakeholders should keep this idea in mind: monocultural education, in the face of our ever-increasing diversity, is irresponsible. Therefore, multicultural education enthusiasts must continue the fight to make the curriculum diverse and inclusive because multicultural education remains integral to the understanding of other cultures and has the potential to counteract racist ideas.

Perhaps one day, the US Department of Education will discard its current standard curriculum in favor of one that is multicultural, complete with best practices that include culturally relevant teaching, which is a pedagogy grounded in the knowledge and display of cultural competence.

MULTICULTURAL EDUCATION LESSON PLANS

Teachers who were educated, from elementary school through college, in a system that promotes a monocultural ideology may have an abbreviated, formal background in multicultural education. For this reason, professional development, including how to create effective lesson plans, is vital to an academic institution where stakeholders are prepared to create and promote a multicultural education through a curriculum that benefits all students.

Listed below are details about the classroom library and the reading survey that may help teachers plan lessons with multiculturalism in mind.

A carefully planned library: Multicultural education unit plans begin with a thoughtfully planned library of multicultural literature and other multicultural materials. Through a carefully planned library of multicultural books and materials, educators can provide stellar multicultural resources that will help motivate students and boost their self-esteem.

The reading survey: A pivotal piece of the classroom library is the reading survey which includes a wish list for books. The survey is the easiest way to get to know students and their cultural backgrounds. The document is an ideal resource to help a teacher gather information that provides the data needed to create a bountiful classroom library. Representing a compilation of books from each student's reading wish list, the library will become an eclectic resource of topics that can spark rich and fruitful lesson plans and student dialogue.

Literacy events: Another benefit of unit planning centered on multicultural education and beginning with reading surveys is the opportunity to improve communication between teachers and families while offering reading events that bridge the generational gap between adults and students. For example, poetry slam nights are events where students and family members share their favorite poems or short literary pieces by writers of color. As part of the event, students can compare the lyrics of contemporary rappers like Tupac Shakur to the poems of legendary poets like Countee Cullen. As a bonus, reading events that include family members offer ways to discover the resources parents are willing to share. In a casual conversation with a student's grandfather, a teacher may find a connection to a Tuskegee Airman or Buffalo Soldier.

The terminology: Teachers can encourage racial tolerance with lessons and activities that help students understand the terminology connected to cultural norms. Similarly, teachers can help students understand terms associated with race, racism, or other social constructs. Books that illustrate racial inequities open a space for dialogue about terms associated with oppression. For example, the images of police brutality bring into question detrimental realities of racism like White privilege. Additionally, students can learn that Black scholars like W. E. B. Du Bois publicly discussed the concept that White people have inherent privileges. However, the term "White privilege" is largely associated with Peggy McIntosh, a scholar who wrote about the idea while a professor at Wellesley College in the 1980s.

Classroom discussions: Multicultural materials provide the opportunity for students to live vicariously. In a book, a student's mind can imagine another life while mentally engaging with fictional characters. Through carefully planned classroom discussions, teachers can engage students in dialogues about fictional characters. In these dialogues, students can discuss hypothetical situations using characters in the book. These conversations may promote racial tolerance and decrease instances of bullying.

HOW TO EMBRACE MULTICULTURAL LITERATURE

When considering multicultural literature, some teachers may bypass books that include subjects or ideas that make them uncomfortable. For example, since many writers of color write from a place of pain, their books often focus on instances of injustice. Additionally, multicultural books may promote cultural norms that contrast a teacher's personal beliefs. How can a teacher promote multicultural literature that may make him feel uncomfortable or underprepared?

The first step a teacher needs to take in promoting multicultural literature is resisting the pull to be the sage on the stage. A successful multicultural classroom is student focused. This connects with the idea of allowing student choice when selecting reading materials. In that spirit, students should have ample opportunities to teach lessons, initiate discussions, make speeches, engage in independent study, and organize activities that promote their book choices.

Creating a personal connection with each student is the next step in embracing multicultural literature. Through a series of one-on-one healthy dialogues, a teacher can become familiar with a student's culture, as well as his likes and dislikes. Similarly, these conversations are the best way for the student to have a better understanding of the teacher as well. This personal connection will help ease the fear of offending a student.

It is true. Many teachers who teach cross-culturally have a fear of offending their students. This fear prevents teachers from sharing multicultural literature with their students. Creating a personal relationship with each student that includes a mutual sense of respect will ease that fear. Similarly, a feeling of mutual respect will prompt the teacher and students to set up norms for the classroom that may include becoming familiar with violent or demeaning language that may prove hurtful to the students or the teacher.

Finally, the teacher must create an opportunity to listen to the stories of students who have encountered injustice. The mantra that states "hurt people hurt people" is a reality that can negatively impact the classroom environment. Often when students feel heard, they begin to heal from racial trauma. However, for some teachers and students who are dealing with racial trauma, talking may not be enough to help them heal from past or recent racial transgressions. Some students may need to seek professional assistance.

A SOCIOLOGICAL APPROACH TO
MULTICULTURAL EDUCATION

As a student of Education, a teacher may be familiar with sociological tools and concepts that can help the teacher encourage and foster the principles of antiracism in the classroom. Entering the classroom with a sociologist's frame of mind will prompt the teacher to value his interpersonal relationships with all students while holding an awareness of systemic racism that sets students of color up for failure.

Taking a sociological approach to multicultural education allows a teacher to consider how society impacts education and vice versa. Through intense observation, a teacher can learn how socio-cultural norms influence the students and the class dynamics. Along with intense observation, the sociologist uses other tools that will prove valuable to the teacher. These tools include anecdotal notes, jottings, and interviews.

The activities below provide ample opportunities to use the tools of a sociologist while examining interpersonal relationships that may be altered by implicit biases. The teacher will see how social constructs impress each student's experience. For example, a wealthy student may experience a school field trip differently than a student facing financial constraints. Finally, the activities prompt both the teacher and students to think critically while questioning common-sense beliefs in the world.

Essentially, approaching the classroom like a sociologist solidifies the teacher's role as a facilitator of learning while encouraging self-evaluation. These fun activities may encourage both teacher and students to find the answers to the following three important questions: (1) How does society shape our values? (2) What are the social forces in the classroom that influence student behaviors? (3) Do we possess the agency to shape ourselves? The answers to these questions will serve as valuable information when selecting relevant multicultural literature for the classroom while helping to solidify the principles of antiracism.

SOCIOLOGICAL IN-CLASS ACTIVITIES

- Puzzles: The teacher should observe and take note of interpersonal interactions and activities like completing complicated puzzles with time restrictions. This activity maximizes the opportunities for community building.
- Class discussions: After setting discussion norms and expectations, divide the class into small groups and discuss the students' responses to fictional accounts of controversial ideas and circumstances. Class discussions

provide occasions where students can analyze instances of racism without fear of targeting fellow classmates.

- Role play: Provide students with scenarios involving complicated societal issues to elicit their possible reactions.
- Social gathering with food: This event is a great way to share culture. A teacher can also observe how students interact with each other in a controlled social environment without the constraints of the classroom.
- Bag of goodies: This activity is another way for a student to share his culture or individuality. After providing each student with a paper sack, invite each student to fill the paper bag with four items that illustrate his life, culture, or individuality.

A PSYCHOLOGICAL APPROACH TO MULTICULTURAL EDUCATION

To help foster an anti-racist society that embraces multiculturalism, teachers and other school stakeholders should possess a keen sense of child development. Developmental psychology is the study of children and how their minds develop over time including the milestones they will reach at certain stages of their lives. The science of developmental psychology provides a teacher with the knowledge needed to understand young minds and why they behave in certain or peculiar ways. The stages of development that relate to the formal school experience include prenatal through early adulthood.

Psychology research confirms that parents play an integral role in the influences and stimuli that impact a child's development. It is important to note, that culture can also influence a child's development since culture encompasses the beliefs, norms, and values of a group of people. With this idea in mind, a teacher needs to be completely cognizant of each student's cultural beliefs and how these beliefs shape the student's ideas.

In the effort to understand each student's culture and psychological development, a teacher can refer to resources by authors who are well versed in the subject. These authors include Brian L. Wright, PhD and Shelly L. Counsell, EdD, scholars and authors of "The Brilliance of Black Boys: Cultivating School Success in the Early Grades"; or William A. Corsaro, scholar and author of books about the sociology of childhood.

Additionally, there is important research in the area of Culturally Responsive Teaching (CRT), which is the pedagogy centered upon the theory that a teacher who is culturally competent will help foster an academic environment conducive to students' success, especially students of color. The pedagogy, which was highly promoted by scholars like Gloria Ladson-Billings and Sonia Nieto, includes seven principles or action items. These items are designed to inspire a teacher to create a safe, nurturing environment for students while building and maintaining healthy relationships built on genuine love and respect for each student's individuality. Listed below are the seven principles and suggested activities that bring the pedagogy into play in the school at large, but especially in the classroom.

Affirm the student's cultural connections: This principle may inspire a teacher to invite students to share traditions, food, and stories relating to their cultural or ethnic roots. The principle also presents the opportunity to watch excerpts from television shows or movies that may illustrate an aspect of a student's culture which he values. The Public Broadcasting Service (PBS) offers a plethora of free videos that provide cultural content. Additionally, school activities, programs, entertainment, and theatrical selections should link directly to the effort to make cultural connections with students.

Project a personable attitude: To fully engage with the principles, the teacher must be personable, approachable, and selfless. An aura of kindness and compassion invites each student to enjoy the teacher's company while feeling comfortable in his own skin. A teacher with an amiable manner will create the comfort level and foundation for sharing in the classroom. A personable teacher may exude a charm that is displayed by smiling when a student enters the classroom, laughing at the student's jokes, vocally greeting the student with exuberance, and offering a listening ear. The student needs to feel the teacher's pleasant demeanor inside and outside of the classroom.

Learning environments are physically and culturally inviting: The school is a place where all students should feel a sense of security and familiarity. All aspects of the school and classroom space contribute to these feelings. When considering this principle, teachers and school stakeholders must make a concerted effort to display posters and artwork that "speak" to each student's individuality. Through the spirit of sharing, school stakeholders can display student artwork, writing, achievements, and photos that celebrate students. Any place a student is welcomed in the school should reflect the student as part of the community.

Reinforce the student's academic development: This principle prompts a teacher to learn best practices for inspiring students to become active and engaged learners in the classroom. Since each child learns differently, it behooves the teacher to create a learning profile for each student. This profile should include the ways each student likes to be acknowledged or celebrated.

Make instructional changes to accommodate learning differences: A culturally responsive teacher makes the concerted effort to understand and meet each student's learning style. When teaching large classes, this principle may be hard to achieve. In some cases, students can be grouped according to learning styles. Additionally, the teacher can provide opportunities for independent learning while taking anecdotal notes on each student's progress. These notes can inform future lesson and assessment plans.

Use effective behavior management skills: A teacher who exudes a friendly demeanor while encouraging mutual respect can lead the class as a mentor who is firm yet fair in feedback and discipline. This principle provides the opportunity for a teacher to develop his classroom management philosophy. For example, how will the teacher communicate that he is firm yet fair to each student? Is the teacher invested in each student and prepared to manage his behaviors in a way that reveals a relationship built on a foundation of love and respect? The best way for a teacher to build a positive and inclusive classroom management philosophy is to begin with an examination of his cultural biases. Similarly, a teacher who is in constant awareness of his triggers and practices emotional intelligence will cut down on the feeling of irritation and dismay that often leads to inappropriate classroom management responses like yelling, sarcasm, and the silent treatment.

Provide opportunities for individuality and positive community interactions: In general, several of the principles, if executed correctly, provide ample opportunities for each student to feel celebrated as an individual while being accepted as a valued member of the group.

CONCLUSION

The standard curriculum, with its monocultural point of view, is difficult to change at the state level, however school stakeholders can impact the school environment with multiculturalism in mind. They can choose multicultural materials, subscribe to culturally responsive teaching principles, and write lesson plans that align with the state standards while keeping diversity or multiculturalism at the center of the school's mission.

Although the standard curriculum does not mandate multicultural education, school stakeholders, through a well-planned classroom library and various classroom activities can encourage multiculturalism while positively influencing students. Including a list of key takeaways and messages from classroom teachers, chapter 9 marks teachers and textbooks as influencers with the potentiality to shape young lives.

Chapter 9

The Key Takeaways

The key takeaway in this book is that multicultural education and its relevant literature should show a "growing repertoire of knowledge, an appreciation for the global intellectual heritage of different disciplines, a balanced learning regime and an apparent willingness or respectful desire to learn more" (Taylor and Hoechsmann 2011, 224). This mindset is vital since a dominant culture will cease to exist by 2055. Given this fact, the need to make complex and interesting depictions of people of color and other non-normative people more widely available is imperative and urgent.

Books featuring intriguing or complex protagonists of color are currently available and suitable for the classroom library. The resources in this book, including the metric, are designed to help educators find and align multicultural books with Pennsylvania state standards. Starting with the reading survey as a resource to create book lists, the teacher can create a classroom library of books that peak any student's interests. When designed with great care and consideration, the classroom library becomes the symbol of cultural celebration and individuality.

Every student wants a teacher who sees him as an individual, values his idiosyncrasies, and appreciates his cultural heritage. That is one reason why students appreciate anti-racist teachers who promise to be allies. Where can school stakeholders find the teachers who will do the anti-racist work needed to establish comprehensive multicultural education programs? The work begins in pre-teacher preparatory programs. College educators must focus their efforts on developing programs that better prepare preservice teachers for the diversity of the twenty-first-century classrooms. This may be difficult since professors or message senders, like all humans, share biased ideas with future educators.

TEACHERS AS MESSAGE SENDERS

Message senders are people and things that provide information to us that we can use to shape our understanding of others, events, and the world. All teachers are message senders who have an awesome and everlasting impact on students. Since this is true, teachers must be keenly aware of what they say to students and the materials they share with them as well. The messages and materials must be carefully considered since it not only represents the teacher's academic repository and background but also his ability to access research and information outside of his own persona.

Teachers are major stakeholders in American schools who have the power to reflect and influence our diverse world. For the sake of all students, it is incumbent on all teachers, especially White teachers to adopt this mentality while remaining keenly aware of their inherent biases and racial consciousnesses. The idea is worth repeating: all teachers and administrators must cast an ally eye on every aspect of their work as facilitators of information or message senders. Furthermore, White teachers must meticulously examine the materials they are selecting with a succinct understanding of how and why they adopt or select certain materials.

Despite institutional racism being a ubiquitous roadblock that can impede a successful multicultural curriculum, through intense professional development, teachers and administrators can work on breaking through instantiations of racism like colorblindness to move to cultural appreciation.

TEXTBOOKS AS MESSAGE SENDERS

Textbooks, an example of materials as message senders, play a major role in the standard curriculum. As hardcopy or digital resources, textbooks are the building blocks of the K–12th grade and college curriculum making the publications essential. Whether as a series or singular printing, textbooks are used for a variety of reasons, including as tools for students and teachers.

In most academic areas of study, the textbook is the collection of knowledge upon which a teacher or professor may base his lesson plans or lectures. Textbooks offer the student an opportunity to participate in guided lessons or learn independently while testing his knowledge at certain intervals.

Textbooks that are part of the standard curriculum are guides to the content knowledge that is fundamental to the core subject to which it aligns. Although this may be true, school stakeholders need to use caution when including textbooks as part of any curriculum. Textbooks often include erroneous and outdated information making the publications dangerous, albeit influential message senders. This fact makes critical literacy an essential skill to learn in school.

The following are important points to consider when including a textbook as part of the course of study.

- In textbooks, publishers include research that is ever changing or fluid and not always suitable for publications that are meant to have long shelf lives.
- One textbook may have over fifty contributors who each have his own biased opinions which he may support with fraudulent or misleading research.
- Although textbooks are reviewed by a team of editors, or textbook review boards, many of these professionals are inundated with texts that are overwhelmingly long forcing editors to skip pages to meet deadlines. This practice leaves room for many typos, grammar mistakes, and erroneous information left unchecked.
- State legislators, lobbyists, and religious groups influence textbook publishers creating additional opportunities for printing skewed information.
- Despite warnings from editorial boards, many publishers often refuse to make necessary changes to textbooks citing impending deadlines or costly reprinting concerns.
- Textbook publishers print false information, incorrectly explained, or water-downed concepts to appease important influencers or special interest groups concerned about political correctness.
- When school stakeholders make textbook decisions, they are entering into agreements that may include contracts associated with other materials relating to the selected texts including workbooks and teacher guides. Reneging on textbook contracts or making alternate selections may prove timely and costly since school stakeholders must discard the rejected texts, and research and select new texts that reflect the scope and sequence of the curriculum. School stakeholders may avoid the process of selecting new texts keeping the rejected textbook selection to save time and money.

THE HIDDEN CURRICULUM

Message senders along with the monocultural curriculum reveals a concerted effort to promote monocultural voices. Compiled by the US Department of Education, and administered by educators in the public school system, which is dominated by White females under thirty years old, the standard curriculum is not informed by people of color. In this system of monocultural viewpoints and ideas, it is easy to consider that a hidden curriculum exists.

A hidden curriculum refers to the values and beliefs that are inadvertently taught as a result of lessons relating to a curriculum built on White supremacy. Furthermore, the standard curriculum, which underscores a hierarchical institution where students are divided by several academic and social constructs including socioeconomic status, is maintained by messages expressed or implied in the curriculum.

The current structure of education and the standard curriculum reveal a conundrum that is supported by a hidden curriculum and detrimental to students of color. In general, students are not encouraged to think critically and question authority; however, White students possess inherent privileges that give them advantages that students of color do not have. This reality makes students of color live in a perpetual state of quandary when they see privileges bestowed on White students that they may be able to attain if they disrupt or question the status quo which they are not taught to do and often punished for the attempts.

Essentially, the standard curriculum and status quo contrasts our diverse nation's reality alerting people to the fact that White people can create entire systems, through omissions and misrepresentations, without the input of the people involved in those systems. This state of affairs seems unethical and inspires psychic disequilibrium. This phenomenon is the feeling that people are describing the world without you in it. For students of color, this feeling often encompasses or acerbates other feelings of loneliness, inadequacy, and failure.

DISRUPTING THE STATUS QUO

In order to disrupt the current educational system, school stakeholders need to implement multicultural education that features multicultural literature and other materials as the foundation. Additionally, school stakeholders need to hire and value teachers who perpetually examine their biases, value diversity, and challenge White privilege and the systemic oppression of racial minorities while promoting quality multicultural literature as a way to combat monoculturalism. What follows this section are interviews with educators who embody this mindset.

TEXTBOX 9.1

Interview with Melissa Alexander, EdD

Undergraduate Degree: Elementary Education, Indiana University of Pennsylvania

Master's Degree: Reading Specialist, Gwynedd Mercy University
Doctorate Degree: Cognitive Studies in Reading, Widener University

Question: Name a book that you believe White teachers could benefit from reading.

Answer: I recommend *White Fragility*, by Robin DiAngelo.

Question: What experiences with multicultural literature did you have growing up?

Answer: Honestly, I cannot remember reading any multicultural literature while growing up. I certainly hope that I am incorrect in this memory. However, growing up in a very small rural town, with very little diversity, leads me to believe my memories may be accurate.

Question: What is your experience with multicultural literature in college? List the classes you took as an undergraduate. Include the classes you had as a graduate as well.

Answer: As an undergraduate student, at Indiana University of Pennsylvania (IUP), I was fortunate to have a few courses that included multicultural literature/education. The first class was called Multicultural Education, which all education majors were required to take. I also was fortunate to be able to enroll in an urban education track, which meant I was required to take three classes focusing on multicultural education and I completed my student teaching in an urban classroom (Philadelphia, PA). Additionally, during the time I attended IUP, all elementary education majors had to complete their first student teaching experience (Sophomore Block) in an inner-city public school in Pittsburg, PA. Furthermore, this class required students to commute to the assigned school on a school bus as a "mobile classroom" to have the opportunity to discuss urban teaching. This time allowed for authentic conversation and broke down many stereotypes that many of us had due to having little to no exposure to urban teaching. I did not have any courses that included multicultural literature in my graduate or doctoral programs.

Question: How did the students in these undergraduate and graduate classes respond during these classes about multicultural literature? What was the racial makeup of these classes?

Answer: Most of my education classes consisted of White female students. I would say the conversations were genuinely positive and provided opportunities for growth. I do believe most students sitting in the classroom had never even thought about multicultural literature because most of the students were not only White and female, but also from rural backgrounds with little experience. I have had conversations, many years past my time as an undergraduate student, with others and we have similar memories of having our "eyes open" to diversity.

Question: How did your professor approach the multicultural literature course? Did the professor seem well informed? Did the professor seem to enjoy teaching the course?

Answer: The three men who developed these courses were so engaging, approachable, and knowledgeable of how to teach about multicultural and diversity topics. They were extremely informed and were very passionate about teaching these courses. The professors also provided a space that was safe for people to discuss information and expand their knowledge. In addition to creating these courses, they also created the urban track for students who specifically desired to teach in an urban location. This provided opportunities to learn more within the classroom, but also experience diverse teaching opportunities before graduating. Unfortunately, this specific urban track and these courses no longer exist at IUP due to two of the professors retiring and budget cuts. I know the professor who is currently teaching fought to keep the program for years, but unfortunately, he was unsuccessful.

Question: Why did you become a teacher? What genres of literature do you enjoy teaching the most?

Answer: I am an elementary teacher and I love teaching the little ones through vibrant picture books/read alouds. I try to include a rich selection of diverse multicultural literature and have these books available for students to read on their own as well. I am always in search of quality, culturally diverse chapter books to read aloud to my students. At this time, I haven't fell in love with the choices that I have read so far. So, the search continues.

Question: Did you ever teach a class with students of diverse backgrounds? Detail your experiences with the different culture.

Answer: Yes. I taught in an inner-city classroom located in North Philadelphia for nine years. The elementary school was a "diamond in the rough" and culturally diverse. I taught students who were Black, Latinx, Middle Eastern, Asian and White. I learned so much and expanded my understanding of people from different cultures. One way I was able to truly learn about my students and their culture was to go to their houses for dinner. My students and families welcomed me with open arms. Also, I attended their neighborhood events, parties, and religious celebrations. These were some of my fondest memories of teaching in Philadelphia.

Question: Did you ever teach multicultural literature to students of color? If so, what were some of the responses you received from the students about the books?

Answer: Yes. I try extremely hard to incorporate multicultural literature in my classroom and received various reactions from my students of color. I specifically remember discussing a story about Elijah McCoy and his development of the steam engine. In this third-grade class of mostly White students, we discussed the word slavery. Most of my students had never been exposed to this word. One of the third graders, a young Black girl, asked to share her knowledge and resources about slavery with the class. She brought in books and a compilation of information that she and her parents put together. It was an amazing experience for her to be able to share her knowledge with the students. They enjoyed receiving a lesson from someone other than me. Since this student was struggling with the traditional work, her experience of being the "teacher" for the day allowed her to gain confidence. As a bonus, the students began to view her as a leader.

Question: How would you describe the schools in which you taught? How are the schools different?

Answer: I taught for nine years in a public inner-city elementary school located in North Philadelphia. For the past seven years I have been teaching in the suburbs in a public suburban elementary school located in Chester County. The differences are incredibly vast. There is a large discrepancy in funding of these two schools: In the suburban school there are student supplies provided by the district, ample educational resources, teacher instruction/support (instructional coaches for staff and support teachers for students), up to date technology, tech instruction and support, and greater opportunities for students in the arts and sciences through optional after school clubs. The demographics and socioeconomics of the students are not the same: The suburban school in which I teach in is predominately White and middle/upper middle class, while the school that I taught at in Philadelphia consisted of mostly Brown and Black students and was 95 percent below the poverty line.

Question: Did you ever teach White students about multicultural literature? If so, what were some of the responses you received from the students about the books? What did you learn from these students about the multicultural literature?

Answer: For the past seven years, I have been teaching multicultural literature to mostly White students. Since my students are young, they absorb new information like sponges. My students love learning about other cultures through literature. I love finding books that normalize and showcase various cultures. For example, I try to find books about children of different cultures going on adventures, celebrating holidays, showing friendships and other "normal" things. We also discuss important public figures such as Martin Luther King, Jr. and Ruby Bridges (etc.); however, I find it extremely important to showcase books with characters of color not specifically showcasing the characteristic "grit" and/or being the handful of public figures that are typically showcased in schools. I am thrilled to see that every year, my White students show a desire to learn more about different cultures and about people of color. Furthermore, many of my students love making personal connections to the books.

Question: As a teacher who identifies as White, what advice would you give to White teachers who are seeking to offer their students multicultural literature or perhaps teaching multicultural literature for the first time?

Answer: I think something that I have been reflecting on about myself from when I was a young, White, naïve, teacher is that I thought I knew everything. I thought after a year or two of "opening my eyes" I had reached the end of learning about diversity. What I now understand is that there is no "end" when discussing multicultural topics. I would encourage White teachers to read, listen and grow from their students, other educators, and books to be able to be the most effective teachers when using multicultural literature in their classrooms. Additionally, I think one of the most important things is to be honest and humble when discussing hard topics. Allowing students to know that you may not have the answer to a question or cannot completely relate to an experience discussed in a book will be powerful to students. It may also allow students who have a real life understanding to be able to discuss their experiences. A teacher who is embarking on a journey of teaching multicultural literature for the first time needs to understand that it may feel very uncomfortable and they may even fear questions from students and parents. For this reason, it is important that a teacher has a deep understanding of the book they are using to instruct from and plans for deep and rich discussion for students to have. Furthermore, the more a teacher uses multicultural literature, the more they will feel comfortable teaching it.

Question: What revelation have you had about multicultural literature?

Answer: I examined non-White female characters in children's picture books for my dissertation. The results were alarming. First, the lack of non-White female characters is extremely upsetting. Second, most non-White female characters were portrayed in a motherly or teaching role. While the roles of mother and teacher are admirable, they are not the only way women of color should be portrayed in children's books. It is vital that female children of color can open children's books and see themselves within the pages. Female children of color need to see the same opportunities for their lives that White children see while reading a book (adventure, sciences, explorer, smart, emotional, etc.). I learned a lot from reading books on racism like *White Fragility* by Robin DiAngelo. This book helped me realize the work I needed to do within myself to understand more of the systemic racism that exists in our nation, especially the school system. I highly recommend this book for anyone, but specifically White people who are interested in learning more and growing in their understanding of racism—specifically their own racism. The benefits of multicultural literature are extremely important from birth and beyond. Studies have shown that children are able to identify race and show racial discrimination as early as three years of age. For this reason, it is imperative that we are providing our youngest readers with books that include characters of color. On the other hand, children of color, need to see themselves doing amazing things within the pages of books. It is normal for White kids to see themselves doing ordinary to extraordinary activities in book (going on adventures, exploring, being scientists, etc.). Furthermore, it is imperative to ensure that most books with characters of color are not shown as activists or poor with "grit." These are the two most common images of characters of color. Teachers need to maintain diversity in their multicultural literature.

TEXTBOX 9.2

Interview with Andrea Kuhar, MEd

Undergraduate Degree: Education, Rutgers University
Master's Degree: University of Pennsylvania

Question: Name two books that you believe White teachers could benefit from reading.

Answer: I enjoy literary fiction, and nonfiction. Two of my recent favorite books are *There, There* by Tommy Orange, and *Born a Crime* by Trevor Noah.

Question: What experiences with multicultural literature did you have growing up?

Answer: Honestly, as a very young person I think my awareness of books with characters that didn't look like me first came from the great LeVar Burton on *Reading Rainbow*. What a gift he is! I was also immersed in the *American Girl* world, and my first ever book signing was when *Meet Addy* came out. Addy was the first Black American girl doll. Her family escaped from slavery to Philadelphia. I also have distinct memories of reading the book *Hiawatha* in first or second grade with my teacher. It was my favorite purchase from the book fair that year.

Question: What is your experience with multicultural literature in college?

Answer: Rutgers mandated that the English majors take an African American literature course. I took Harlem Renaissance and Jazz as Literature, which prioritized Black voices. I had a wonderful teacher who was an expert in the genre of graphic novels. She brought the experience of Black women to the forefront. I also took a class in Korean literature which I really enjoyed.

Question: How did the professor or students in these undergraduate and graduate classes respond during these classes about multicultural literature? What was the racial makeup of these classes?

Answer: I have a distinct memory of thinking our Jazz in Literature teacher hated our class. He had long dreadlocks and was soft spoken. Our class, which was mostly White, was so quiet. When the professor asked us questions like "What makes this an authentic black experience?" The question would hang in the air and there'd just be crickets chirping. I think the group of eighteen- to twenty-one-year-old students were not sure how to respond to that question at the time. This made the professor irritated if not angry. I remember seeing this professor outside of class and I was shocked at how warm he was toward me and a classmate. I do remember watching "Many Rivers to Cross" with Jimmy Cliff in this class. I was mesmerized by the music. Jimmy Cliff remains a constant on my playlists even now! My Korean Literature teacher was absolutely an expert, and I enjoyed her very much. I remember that this class had a majority of White students and the worst behaved undergrad classes I had in my undergraduate career.

Question: How did your professor approach the multicultural literature course? Did the professor seem well informed? Did the professor seem to enjoy teaching the course?

Answer: In both the Jazz as Literature and the Korean Literature course, there was a disconnect between the students and the teacher—and this led to a really superficial survey of some books that I believe were quite powerful. The professors were absolutely experts. The students, mostly White, had no idea how to engage with discussions on race. In the case of Korean Literature, some unfortunate members of the student body didn't believe their experience connected with the class in any way.

Question: Why did you become an English teacher? What literary works do you enjoy teaching the most?

Answer: In college, I kept choosing English education classes because I just loved them. At some point, I realized that my teachers were some of the smartest, most insightful, most creative people I knew. I wanted to be that way also and that is why I became an English teacher. I had a really fun experience teaching *Romeo and Juliet* by William Shakespeare this year. I love to teach Shakespeare, and believe his themes are still relevant even in 2020. Previously, I taught James McBride's *The Color of Water*, which I really loved teaching. The students related to McBride as a young man of color, and they also connected to Ruth, his White mother.

Question: Did you ever teach a class with students of diverse backgrounds? Detail your experiences with the different cultures.

Answer: I taught for five years in a small charter school with students from the Black diaspora. The students were Christian, and Muslim, and I even had a student who recently emigrated from Jamaica. I loved my experience working with these students, but sometimes it was extremely challenging to get all students to engaged in my class. Relationship building was very important—I learned a great deal about myself, teaching, and my students throughout my time there.

Question: Did you ever teach students of color about books in the Western canon? If so, what are some of the responses you received from the students? What did you learn from these students about the Western canon?

Answer: My first year, I taught *Othello* by Shakespeare. That was the last time I taught Shakespeare at this school. I would have been more successful if I taught excerpts instead of reading it from beginning to end. We also read *I Hear America Singing* by Walt Whitman and paired it with *I, Too, Sing America* by Langston Hughes. That was a fascinating comparison and well received by students.

Question: Did you ever teach White students about multicultural literature? If so, what were some of the responses you received from the students about the books? What did you learn from these students about the multicultural literature?

Answer: In 2020, prior to the murder of George Floyd, I taught *A Raisin in the Sun* by Lorraine Hansberry at a school that is predominantly White, and approximately 30 percent Black. Since I like to be explicit in my teaching, I paired the play with a lesson on redlining. I made this decision because I didn't learn about redlining until my adult years. I wanted to share this information with my students. My students' responses were incredible. They had a great deal of emotion and insight about the Younger family, as well as heartfelt reactions to learning about redlining. We watched a PBS documentary called "Where does the American Dream Live?" The perspectives became crucial to my students' understanding of the human experience in America.

Question: As a teacher who identifies as White, what revelation have you had about multicultural literature?

Answer: When White teachers are prepared to teach multicultural literature, they should dive right in! There is incredible YA fiction literature available that students will enjoy. The same is true for historical fiction. A phrase that's been playing in my head recently is *African American History IS American History*. The same is true for Native American, Asian American, and a great deal of other identities as well. Another revelation I had over the years is that students deserve the very best of every genre—and they deserve a diverse makeup of authors, writers, and artists in the classroom. I don't think we should look at a group of Black students and say "Forget all White authors." I just think our students deserve the very best of everything. Multiple perspectives are extremely valuable. Student experiences should be reflected in what they are reading, but they should also be gaining perspectives outside of their own experience. This is exactly the right time to make the shift.

TEXTBOX 9.3

Multidimensional Identities in Literature

When I think of multicultural literature, I think of how students' identities are portrayed. I go back to the high school where I taught English to speakers of other languages. Someone walking through the halls of the school might see diversity in terms of skin color or they might hear diversity in the multitude of languages spoken by the students. The English learners had a more nuanced perspective on diversity and the portrayal of their identity in multicultural literature. When they selected books, the English learners sought out stories that reflected their multidimensional identities as teenagers coming of age. They sought confirmation on who they were and inspiration on who they could be.

The literacy practices of these adolescent readers shaped my view on multicultural literature. They did not want me to see them as a one-dimensional stereotype. Just because a book featured a Spanish-speaking adolescent did not ensure it was a rich, accurate portrayal. Some of the English learners' reading choices reflected their unique past, such as crossing an international border. Many sought out stories about their own situations with relationships and resiliency. Others saw themselves in the protagonist of a science fiction story in which an everyday teen becomes the hero. Like myself as a reader, they read to reflect on who they were, who they are today, and who they could be in the future.

I also learned about reading choices through formal research. I conducted a study at the school on the English learners' literacy engagement in the English department's choice reading program. This was a dream environment for engaging adolescents in literacy. The classroom shelves were stocked with new titles, and the librarian borrowed books from other schools. The students became critical consumers of fiction and nonfiction. The findings of this study indicated that the most popular genre was "coming of age." The English learners, male and female, found themselves represented in this human experience. Their lives were on the page. It was exciting to discover that the students created a community in this physical and temporal space to talk about books and relate them to each other's lives. Having a choice in what to read is powerful for adolescents if we offer a broad selection of literature, which speaks to their multidimensional identities.

From my years as a teacher and researcher, I have a deeper appreciation of each reader's distinctive identities. Adolescents are not a monolithic population. I remember early in my teaching career the enthusiasm of school districts to purchase multicultural literature as a new genre. Regrettably, our critical literacy skills to evaluate these titles lagged behind the deluge from publishers that quickly filled our shelves. Today, we have the responsibility to seek out books that do not perpetuate stereotypes or marginalization. I have learned that just because a book has a particular character or context, it does not automatically get a space on the shelf.

Michelle Ohanian, PhD
Assistant Professor of Education School of Education

TEXTBOX 9.4

The Fierce Urgency of Now: The Importance of Multicultural Literature in U.S. Schools and Classrooms

"The fierce urgency of now" was a phrase that the Reverend Dr. Martin Luther King Jr. articulated several times in his speeches and writings. For example, in his famous "Beyond Vietnam" sermon, which was delivered at the Riverside Church in New York City on April 4, 1967, exactly one year before he was executed in Memphis, TN, Dr. King shared: "We are now faced with the fact that tomorrow is today. We are confronted with the fierce urgency of now. In this unfolding conundrum of life and history there is such a thing as being too late."

It is within the lens of "the fierce urgency of now" that we also have to wrestle with the current realities within too many US schools and classrooms. Specifically, we are still dealing with the history of racism, White supremacy, patriarchy, sexism, xenophobia, transphobia, ableism, and homophobia within society that also slithers into school districts, schools, and classrooms on a daily basis. Thus, too many teachers and educational leaders struggle to deal with the "elephant in the school and classroom," while simultaneously providing diverse students with multicultural literature that could provide a counternarrative to the hegemonic school system that fails to holistically value their humanity.

This is why a commitment to equity (not equality) advocates and demands teachers and educational leaders understand the importance of books as mirrors, in which all students' identities, traditions, and communities are positively revealed and cherished. Sadly, the aforementioned has not pervasively occurred. Explicitly within society and schools, we are dealing with what Dr. Eddie Glaude (2016) would term a "value gap," which is the value we place on White people (and White culture) in comparison to others.

In his influential book, *The Souls of Black Folk*, W. E. B. Du Bois (1903) offers a forerunner analysis to Dr. Glaude's "value gap" by declaring:

> Between me and the other world there is ever an unasked question: unasked by some through feelings of delicacy; by others through the difficulty of rightly framing it. All, nevertheless, flutter round it. They approach me in a half-hesitant sort of way, eye me curiously or compassionately, and then, instead of saying directly, How does it feel to be a problem? They say, I know an excellent colored man in my town; or, I fought at Mechanicsville; or, do not these Southern outrages make your blood boil? At these I smile, or am interested, or reduce the boiling to a simmer, as the occasion may require. To the real question, How does it feel to be a problem? I seldom answer a word. (Du Bois 1903, 7–8).

In order for "all" US students to experience a sense of belonging, feel valued, and not depicted as "problems," it is imperative that teachers, educational leaders, and librarians are committed to the "fierce urgency of now," as it relates to bringing multicultural literature into the classroom.

Within my own professional practice, I made it my life's calling to challenge both preservice and in-service teachers to understand that multicultural literature provides students with various voices, which is critical to one's understanding of the world! For example, my worldview, passions, and personal pursuits changed because of my exposure to the works of

Langston Hughes, James Baldwin, Richard Wright, Malcolm X, Ralph Ellison, bell hooks, Jawanza Kunjufu, and Naim Akbar. Therefore, I am convinced that students will experience a similar internal revival when we provide and expose them to the beauty and brilliance of multicultural literature.

In this critically important book: *Turning the Page: The Ultimate Guide for Teachers to Multicultural Literature*, Dr. Rachel Slaughter challenges preservice teachers, in-service teachers, educational leaders, librarians, and educational equity advocates on "the fierce urgency of now," as it pertains to multicultural literature in schools and classrooms. And in doing so, perhaps, we are closer to *Turning the Page* to a more auspicious future in schools and classrooms that will include multicultural voices in the American canon.

Dr. Ronald W. Whitaker, II, EdD

Culturally Responsive Assistant Professor of Education and Co-Founding Director of the Center for Urban Education, Equity, and Improvement at Cabrini University

CONCLUSION

While school stakeholders may have an awareness of global diversity, cultural differences, or multicultural images are not widely included in the standard curriculum. In order to reverse this reality, educators must make a commitment to select and disseminate materials that respect the differences among people while embracing multiculturalism.

Since educational bias is prevalent in schools, educators need tools that will inform their decisions when selecting materials appropriate for the classroom. Such tools are essential given the evidence that erroneous information is rife in academic materials, including textbooks that underscore racist ideas and a hidden curriculum. For the sake of vulnerable and impressionable young minds, these messages need to be canceled.

To further distance themselves from academic materials that are counterintuitive to multicultural education, educators will need to seek out opportunities for professional development where they learn to appreciate the genre while practicing ways of how to appropriately share it with their students. Sharing experiences by and about people of color will lead us to celebrating what Dr. Whitaker calls "the beauty and brilliance of multicultural literature."

Chapter 10

The Reading QUILT Book Reviews and Lesson Plans

The process of teachers recommending books to students is a wonderful way to make teacher-student connections. Starting with a book survey and continuing with dialogue or reflection journals, chat rooms, and book chats, book recommendations help solidify a personal connection with each student.

In the digital world, book selections are easier than ever. Starting with a quick search on the internet, students can find books that fit the genre of their choice. For a deeper dive into each book, teachers and students can access sites like Goodreads, Bookbub, and Epic Reads. These sites list comprehensive summaries of books that may interest readers. Additionally, there are websites that include curated lists of multicultural books. Sites like Children's Book Council, Parents, Families and Friends of Lesbian, Gay, Bisexual and Transgender People (PFLAG), and Diversity in YA can help teachers and students find the perfect book.

Book recommendations are an ideal teaching tool. Besides an opportunity for teachers to stretch their interests and teaching skills, book recommendations open a world of reading and writing activities. Here are a few literacy activities that may spark reading in middle through high school grade levels.

- Journaling: A journal is a book where a student can compile his feelings about daily events and respond to ideas he read in a book. A dialogue journal is a book where a student can write his feelings about a book and request a response from a friend or teacher.
- Faux Facebook: To illustrate characterization, a student can create Facebook pages for characters which can include each character's "friend" list, posts, and plot elements that the character's friends "liked."
- Character debates: Choose two characters from the same book or pair two characters from different books to engage in a friendly debate.

- Downward spiral chart: Using a character's decisions, create a flow chart or graphic that shows the character's moral or emotional decline.
- Create a soundtrack: Using the literary elements of the book, a student can find song lyrics that represent the book's characters, plot, setting, and theme.
- Poetry slam: Like the soundtrack, a student can find poems that represent the books literary elements.

CORE STANDARDS

Created to guarantee that all students are prepared for various post-graduate jobs or academic experiences, the Common Core State Standards established comprehensive guidelines detailing what students need to know in core subjects like history, math, and English language arts from kindergarten through twelfth grade.

Written by academic experts from across the country, the Common Core focuses on developing critical and analytical skills that students need to learn to succeed in this ever-changing world. Forty-one states, the District of Columbia, four territories, and the Department of Defense Education Activity (DoDEA) have voluntarily adopted the standards. These standards are included in the book reviews featuring the QUILT metric.

THE READING QUILT MULTICULTURAL
BOOK REVIEWS AND CORE STANDARDS

Multicultural literature is an essential building block of a multicultural education program. A teacher who is diligent in finding quality multicultural literature suitable for the classroom needs to be meticulous in his lesson planning in order to bring the book alive in the classroom while aligning the book to academic standards. Using the Common Core State Standards as a guide, teachers can incorporate multicultural literature into their lesson plans while adhering to academic standards outlined for their respective states.

"The Reading Quilt" book reviews provide short reviews of books that a teacher may use to spark conversations about culture and race, along with learning activities that may help students understand the complexity of the human experience. The book review format includes the acronym QUILT.

Qualities like good writing, universal theme, and well-developed plots represent three important elements of quality multicultural literature.

REALISTIC FICTION

Realistic fiction, a popular literary genre, features stories that mimic real life making the genre an attractive choice for educators and readers of all ages who are curious about human nature and how to maneuver in this complicated world. However, with topics that range from police brutality to mail-order brides, realistic fiction marketed for the adolescent or young adult reader can be a tricky choice for the classroom. Incorporating certain realistic fiction titles in the classroom may invite mature subjects into the classroom that teachers are not prepared to discuss.

Teachers recommend realistic fiction titles to students more often than other genres. In haste, teachers may be tempted to include titles in their reading repertoire without previewing the books. Realistic fiction has many benefits which makes the extra step of previewing the selections worth the effort. Studies show that the genre is perfect for inspiring reluctant readers to consider reading as a fun way to pass the time. Young readers are fascinated by the imaginative way an author spins a story with realistic subtexts. Curious how the protagonist will deal with a problem that the reader could experience makes realistic fiction stimulating and engrossing.

The genre includes themes like "coming of age," "good and evil," "racism" and "survival," lending itself well to cross curricular lesson plans. To offer selections that include topics which are age-appropriate, teachers can check sources like Book Wizard powered by Scholastic. Along with other cool tidbits of information about the book, this amazing resource helps you check the reading level and theme of a selected book. Several realistic fiction books are recommended in this chapter.

SNATCH: THE ADVENTURES OF DAVID AND ME IN OLD NEW YORK

Snatch: The Adventures of David and Me in Old New York (Philadelphia: David and Me Publishing, Inc., 2010) is a historical fiction novella written by Charles Fuller, a native of Philadelphia. Fuller, a native of north Philadelphia, is the Pulitzer Prize–winning playwright of *A Soldier's Play*.

Charles Fuller

A prolific writer, Fuller was born in Philadelphia in 1939 and attended local schools like Roman Catholic High School, Villanova University, and LaSalle University. In fact, it was in Roman Catholic High School that Fuller first lit his passion to become a writer. Dismayed at the lack of books by Black authors in his high school's library, Fuller vowed to become an author who could represent his culture.

Quality: In *Snatch: The Adventures of David and Me in Old New York*, Fuller introduces his young readers to two brothers David and Charles, "free" Black kids who live in the Five Points neighborhood of antebellum New York City in 1838. Five Points, which was in Lower Manhattan, included streets like Cross and Little Water and a five-point intersection is named as "the principal stop on the Underground Railroad in New York." The modern Five Points section is now Chinatown.

With NYC as the backdrop, David and Charles, always on the hunt for adventure, meet a fugitive slave named Freddie Johnson who they help elude a gang of slave catchers led by a mysterious man called "Snatch." The boys' wild adventure spans thirty-six hours and features turmoil in the tunnels of Old New York, witches, a gang fight, and a big reveal.

Universal theme: Fuller, skilled at bringing history alive, captures the spirit of the two brothers and their quest to protect a fugitive slave. Told in first-person point of view, the novel features characters with cool nicknames and historical icons that young people can research as part of a history lesson. A discussion of "Ole'-Hit-You-With-A-Switch Moses Bowman," the boy's teacher in the Colored Free School, could spark a classroom conversation about racially segregated schools and the desire for African American families to educate their children before, during, and after slavery. Complete with a teacher's guide written by Marguerite Tiggs Birt, the novel is the perfect addition to a middle school history curriculum.

Imaginative plot: Fuller's novel will take a young reader on a romp that may postpone his social media engagement for a day or two. Through clues, a rousing chase, and near-death experiences, the book underscores the theme of "freedom." In the novel, the two protagonists, Charles and David, protect each other through thick and thin while teasing at the same time. The familial bond and brotherly affection will endear the brothers to the reader.

Lesson plan: Since the genre of realistic fiction includes fictionalized historical accounts, it may include real and recognizable iconic images, historical figures, and facts that can lead a student into a great research project.

Talking points: Fuller's novel provides the platform to discuss important historical information from the time period.

- What is meant by Old New York?
- Who were the slave catchers and why were they needed?
- What methods did slave catchers use to catch slaves who tried to run to freedom?
- Who helped the slaves find freedom?

Standard areas 9.2, 9.3, CC.1.2: Historical and cultural context and critical response and reading informational texts: As part of the lesson, students can read, understand, and respond to the novel while discussing the talking points and comparing the historical informational to first- and second-hand accounts of the experiences. This textual comparison emphasizes comprehension, making connections among ideas and between texts with focus on textual evidence.

Vocabulary preview: Before reading the text, the teacher can preview words and concepts like slave catcher, Colored Free School, Old New York, elude, segregation, Colored Free Schools, and fugitive slaves.

UP FROM SLAVERY

Important note: The novel *Up from Slavery* (New York: Bantam, 1901) includes the use of the n-word in historical context. Teachers, please discuss, with your students, the school's policy on saying the n-word in the academic setting.

Up from Slavery (New York: Bantam, 1901) is Booker T. Washington's autobiography. In his book, Washington shows the readers that there is no sweeter taste than that of freedom, and when your freedom is merely a wish or memory, you die a little inside for every moment you are not free.

Washington's masterpiece describes the institution of slavery, which lasted over four centuries. Slavery, the cruelty that enslaved nearly 60 million African people, was a legal and widely celebrated institution. It is in this state of cruelty, where more than 4 million men, women, and children died in horrific ways. Despite the inclusion of slavery's history in the American curriculum, few people can hardly visualize the days and nights of the enslaved victims who endured what Dr. John Henrik Clarke describes succinctly as the time when Africans were "torn from their homeland, herded onto ships, and dispersed all over the so-called New World." Torn, herded, and dispersed, it is in the unpacking of these verbs where the true crime against humanity is detailed.

After many years, slavery officially ended on June 19. Affectionately called "Juneteenth," the name refers to the day in 1865 when the slaves received the message that their freedom was granted.

Booker T. Washington

Booker T. Washington was born on April 5, 1856, in Hale's Ford, Franklin County, Virginia, where the name of Taliaferro, Booker's middle name, was associated with prominent people who settled in Virginia in the seventeenth century. Booker's birth to Jane, a slave cook, and a White man, signifies Booker's compromised and violent beginning. Specifically, Booker was born a slave and grew up on the James Burroughs tobacco plantation, where Booker's mother was the cook. Originally named Booker Taliaferro, Jane decided later to erase that name from Booker's future.

When Booker was just a baby, Jane, a new mother, met and fell in love with a slave named Washington Ferguson. Jane and Washington married. Later the couple conceived Amanda, and other children while preparing Booker for a life on his own.

Before starting his formal academic journey, he gave himself the name "Washington" out of respect to Washington Ferguson. Nine years later, the small family left Burrough's farm to start a life with Washington Ferguson who needed to leave for work on a salt farm in Malden, Virginia, when Booker was a small boy.

Shortly after his stepfather arrived in Malden, Booker joined his stepfather packing salt at just nine years old. At the tender age of ten, Booker, a hard worker, began working in a coal mine while going to school. Along with the work in the coal mines, Booker took a job with General Lewis Ruffner, owner of the mines, as Mrs. Ruffner's houseboy.

Quality: In his book, Booker details significant life experiences as a slave. Originally published in a magazine titled *Outlook*, Booker, encouraged by readers, gathered the vignettes together to publish an autobiography of forty years of his life. In the book's preface, Booker shows a humility about his life's work and literary success giving accolades to his Tuskegee colleague Max Bennett Thrasher. Thrasher, four years his junior, was also an accomplished writer.

Universal theme: The theme of industriousness is a prominent and inspirational one in this novel of profound personal fortitude. With chapter headings like "A Slave among Slaves," "The Struggle for Education," and "Early Days at Tuskegee," the narrative speaks to people who understand education as a personal freedom and escape from mental slavery. Quoted as saying, "success is to be measured not so much by the position that one has reached in life as by the obstacles which he has overcome," Booker hoped his autobiography would inspire other people to courageously embrace the productive struggle.

Imaginative story: The book opens with the chapter "A Slave among Slaves," which is an account of Booker's life as a slave. In his book, Booker writes about his life using descriptive language or imaginative metaphors. He writes that he learned of his African ancestors and the atrocities the African people endured on the middle passage of the slave ship while being conveyed from Africa to America through "secrets and whispers."

Lesson plan: Slavery in the United States was a reality from the seventeenth through the nineteenth centuries. The "legal institution of human chattel enslavement" helped the United States move into economic stability using free labor. Slaves maintained plantations and tended crops like tobacco and cotton while tending to the plantation owners' personal lives as butlers, maids, houseboys, chambermaids, and cooks. A lesson may center on the individual lives of slaves whose existence tell their stories of dauntlessness, grit, spirituality, and perseverance. Other lessons may include the tenacity of the slaves and their fight for freedom.

Talking points: Historians tell us that the American curriculum has compromised the timeline and personal stories of slavery and the slaves. If this is true, do Americans know the real history of slavery?

- What is your understanding of the institution of slavery?
- Is it important to remember the stories of individual slaves like Booker T. Washington? If so, which slave's story do you know well?
- What part of Booker's story resonates with you? What lessons did the autobiography teach you?

Standard areas 9.2, 9.3, CC.1.2: Historical and cultural context and critical response and reading informational texts: As part of the lesson, students can read, understand, and respond to the novel while discussing the talking points and comparing the historical informational to first- and second-hand accounts of the experiences. This textual comparison emphasizes comprehension, making connections among ideas and between texts with focus on textual evidence.

Vocabulary preview: Before reading the text, the teacher can preview words and concepts like slavery, philanthropy, liberal, and freedom.

THE HOUSE ON MANGO STREET

In her novel *The House on Mango Street* (New York: Vintage, 1991), Sandra Cisneros shares her experiences of her home with vivid imagery. In chapters like "Louie, His Cousin, and His Other Cousin" and "Cathy Queen of Cats," we experience Esperanza's world through poignant and insightful vignettes that give the reader snippets of her life as a Latina coming of age in the poorest part of Chicago.

Sandra Cisneros

The House on Mango Street, Cisneros' first novel, helped her gain acclaim as a gifted vignette writer. Born in Chicago, Illinois, on December 20, 1954, Cisneros was the third of seven children. Cisneros parents Alfredo Cisneros del Moral and Elvira Cordero Anguiano raised Sandra and her siblings in Chicago. When Cisneros was eleven years old her family moved to Humboldt Park, a predominantly Puerto Rican area that became the inspiration for *The House on Mango Street*.

While attending a Catholic girls' high school, Cisneros met a teacher who inspired her to write poetry. Her love for poetry bloomed in college where she began to explore her intersectionality of being a female Mexican American.

Quality of writing: In the novel, Cisneros offers a window into the life of Esperanza Cordero, a young girl living in impoverished Chicago. With stark honesty and colloquial language, Cisneros paints a collage of people and circumstances she encounters in her neighborhood. In her authentic descriptions, the reader is privy to her mixed bag of feelings. Like a buffet, Cisneros offers shame, pride, and disdain in episodic notes that leave the reader thoughtful.

Universal theme: The coming-of-age theme is a popular one in young adult fiction. In the novel, Esperanza's keen exploration of her life and culture is proof of her budding adulthood. Conversely, sometimes, with child-like eyes, Esperanza details adult encounters that leave the reader feeling sorry for her. This is true when an old Asian man kisses her full on the mouth without her consent.

Imaginative plot: Cisneros' sketches of Esperanza Cordero describe a year of her life. In that year, Esperanza moved into a broken-down palace on Mango Street. To Esperanza's dismay, it is her parents' pride and the object of her disdain. At twelve years old, while living on Mango Street, Esperanza meets her neighbors and experiences their idiosyncratic behaviors. In a poetic style, Cisneros reveals Esperanza's encounters with poverty, sex, and sexual assault. In the end, Cisneros leaves her neighborhood, but carries Mango Street and "the ones that cannot out" in her psyche.

Lesson plan: As the child of a Mexican father and a Mexican American mother, Sandra Cisneros bounced back and forth between Mexico and the United States. In lessons about the novel, students can learn the history of Mexico's relationship with the United States, and what it means to be Mexican American.

Talking points:
- What terms are used in reference to Mexican people? Can you explain terms like "Latino," "Chicano," "Hispanic," "Mexican descent," and "Mexican American"?

- What is the history of the Mexican-United States border? Describe the controversies and disputes relating to this border.
- How are Mexican Americans and people of Mexican descent portrayed in the media?
- How do these images affect your feelings about Mexican Americans or their culture?

Standards areas CC.1.2.8: Cite the textual evidence that most strongly supports an analysis of what the text says explicitly, as well as inferences, conclusions, and/or generalizations drawn from the text: A student can choose an idea included in the plot like Mexican-United States border relations. Using the idea, a student can state an assertion while choosing textual evidence to support it.

Vocabulary preview: Before reading the text, the teacher can preview words and concepts like immigration, migration, and emigration.

THE WATSONS GO TO BIRMINGHAM—1963

The Watsons Go to Birmingham—1963 (New York: Yearling, 1997), written by Christopher Paul Curtis, is a favorite choice in school libraries and bookstores across the country.

Family is an integral part of the African American culture often celebrated in pop culture television shows and movies like *Everybody Hates Chris*, *Blackish*, and *Soul Food*. These shows epitomize the strong African American mother who is eclipsed by the stronger African American grandmother both flanked by supportive husbands, precocious children, and nosey aunts and uncles. The African American family, depicted in the media in myriad ways, is iconic.

Fans laugh at the silly sitcoms of the African American family on TV, but do the media images hold some semblance of truth? We see the staunch, yet regal, hardworking mother who is the mouthpiece of the family, quick to throw her house shoe at her "smart mouth" kids. She is sassy on her own, but a force to be reckoned with when her sisters show up only to give lip service to the husband who gets the big piece of chicken at family dinner.

When carefully considered, these images of the African American family illustrate integral family values, the most prevalent being "family is paramount." This motto, along with the classic and sometimes comical images of the African American family, has a long history and a prominent place in the African American culture. Christopher Paul Curtis epitomizes the African American family in his novel *The Watsons Go to Birmingham—1963*.

Christopher Paul Curtis

Curtis was born to a podiatrist father and teacher mom in Flint, Michigan, on May 10, 1953. The oldest of five siblings, he is the author of a host of books that feature Flint. Curtis's book put Flint in the minds of many young readers, but the city, which is 66 miles northwest of Detroit, is now on our minds for the Flint water crisis, just one of the many tragedies Flint residents have endured. Americans also know Flint as the "automobile manufacturing powerhouse" that fell to ruins in the 1980s, and the subsequent crime explosion that pushed the government officials to call a state of financial emergency in 2002.

In the early 1970s, at nineteen years old, Curtis graduated from Flint Southwestern High School and enrolled in Flint University of Michigan founded in 1956. Hoping to fund his college education and secure his future, Curtis landed a job at Fisher Body Plant established in 1908. His hard work as a blue-collar factory worker did not overshadow his intellectual abilities. He spent a lot of time at the plant reading and writing on his breaks. Bud Caldwell of the novel *Bud, Not Buddy* was born while Curtis was on the factory line. Curtis, who resides in Detroit, continues to write books for young readers.

Quality: In his book, Curtis introduces his readers to the Watson family. A classic tale of family values, the book won three prestigious awards including the John Newbery Medal, the Golden Kite Award, and the Coretta Scott award "given annually to outstanding African American authors and illustrators of books for children and young adults that demonstrate an appreciation of African American culture and universal human values."

Universal theme: The theme of family is poignant in this novel. The narrative resonates with family who love each other, but erupt in crazy arguments every other day, revealing a familial bond that cannot be broken despite it being tested.

Imaginative plot: The book opens with Byron Watson, a spitfire of a boy who often misuses his "smarts" in dumb ways. Freezing his lips to the mirror of the family's new car is just one example. His younger brother Kenny is witness to the foolishness that Byron spins daily. One day, Mr. and Mrs. Watson decide that Byron breaks the proverbial camel's back, and they vow to take his delinquent stupid self to his petite, aging grandmother who lives in Flint, Michigan. It is during the family's travels that they find themselves amid a tragedy: The Sixteenth Avenue Baptist Church burning.

Lesson plan: The Sixteenth Avenue Baptist Church burning was the hateful act of white supremacists that killed four beautiful girls between the ages of eleven and fourteen. The book is the perfect complement to a lesson about the bombing of the church. A lesson may center on the lives of the four girls: Addie Mae Collins, Cynthia Wesley, Carole Robertson, and Denise McNair.

Talking points: In his novel, Curtis offers the human experience behind the violence that plagued 1963. Known as the defining year of the Civil Rights Movement, the book includes historical elements that could spark a lively discussion.

- What is White supremacy?
- Who were the key leaders who stood up against messages of hate during the Civil Rights Movement?
- Why was the family's car "The Brown Bomber" such an iconic image and an important one to include in the story?
- What are the Watson's family values? And how do the family's values mirror the civil rights movement?

Standard areas 9.2, 9.3, CC.1.2: Historical and cultural context and critical response and reading informational texts: As part of the lesson, students can read, understand, and respond to the novel while discussing the talking points and comparing the historical informational to first- and second-hand accounts of the experiences. This textual comparison emphasizes comprehension, making connections among ideas and between texts with a focus on textual evidence.

Vocabulary preview: Before reading the text, the teacher can preview words, concepts, and events like civil rights, the Sixteenth Avenue Baptist Church burning, emulate, geographical accents, pomade, segregation, boycotts, discrimination, and provoke.

KITCHEN

Despite school officials' best efforts to curb the behavior, homophobia and transphobia are irrational feelings and discriminatory practices that continue to spread like mold in many schools, hindering adolescent development, and threatening lives. For example, statistics show that more than 80 percent of young trans people report being victims of verbal shaming or violent attacks. These harmful experiences can lead to thoughts of suicide or self-harm. Despite this reality, the subjects of homophobia and transphobia are not discussed in books. Essentially, the subjects are taboo in the publishing industry.

Banana Yoshimoto

Kitchen (New York: Grove Press, 2015) by Banana Yoshimoto is translated by Megan Backus. Mahoko Yoshimoto, who created the pseudonym Banana

Yoshimoto, is a Japanese writer who was born in Tokyo on July 24, 1964. Inspired by their famous father Takaaki Yoshimoto, both Mahoko and her older sister Yoiko Haruno, a famous *mangaka*, or comic book author, delight millions of people with their creativity. A former waitress, Mahoko names American authors Stephen King and Truman Capote as writers who influenced her. *Kitchen* is Yoshimoto's debut work which depicts homophobia and bully.

Quality of writing: *Kitchen,* which was made into a movie in 1997, presents Mikage, the heroine, as a lonely young adult orphan who is enchanted by kitchens, the center of the home and her heart. Yoshimoto's writing reads like an ode to kitchens, and the tranquility the room represents. She uses that same poetic energy to immortalize the character Eriko Tanabe, a transgender person who dies at the hands of hateful people.

Universal theme: Mikage, who is already dealing with the death of her beloved grandmother, is hit with the devastating blow of losing Eriko, her friend and confidante, revealing the novel's theme of love's endurance in the face of tragedy.

Imaginative plot: Struggling to overcome her grandmother's death, Mikage uses Yuichi Tanabe as a port in her storm exposing her arrested development. Throughout the story, Mikage navigates her world like Alice in Wonderland, confused by the shenanigans the adult world has to offer.

Lesson plan: This novel provides an opportunity for upper school students to discuss a person's gender identity or gender expression that differs from their sex assigned at birth.

Talking points: Students may benefit from understanding the various terms associated with sexual identity or expression. The following are topics that students can research and discuss as a class.

- Terms associated with transgender identity
- Statistics and stories detailing the lives of transgender people who have died as a result of hate crimes
- Homophobia and how the discrimination presents at school

Standard areas CC.1.2.11–12.C: Analyze the interaction and development of a complex set of ideas, sequence of events, or specific individuals over the course of the text: Using the circumstances in the book, a student can analyze the feelings and circumstances that led Mikage to sleep on Yuichi's amazing couch.

Vocabulary preview: Before reading the text, the teacher can preview words and concepts like bullying, transgender, homophobic, transphobic, and hate crimes.

LITTLE FIRES EVERYWHERE

In the novel *Little Fires Everywhere* (London: Penguin Books, 2017), Celeste Ng, *New York Times* best-selling author, introduces us to a cast of characters with lots of secrets. In this novel, secrets are kept close to the vest. Perpetuated by lies, the family secrets become the catalyst for disaster. This is especially true for Mia Warren, a transient artist and gentle soul, who drives her secret to Shaker Heights, Ohio, in the passenger seat of her tan Volkswagen, shaking up the idyllic affluent suburban neighborhood of Shaker Heights.

Celeste Ng

Celeste Ng, an American author, was born in Pittsburgh, PA. She also spent some time in Shaker Heights, Ohio, a suburb of Cleveland. Warrensville Township, a location featured in Ng's book, is southeast of Cleveland. The first settlers arrived in the wooded area in 1808.

A graduate of Harvard, Celeste went on to earn an MFA at the University of Michigan. Her writing career began with essays, which were met with accolades and awards while appearing in publications like *New York Times* and *The Guardian*. Celeste's first novel *Everything I Never Told You* (London: Penguin Books, 2014) was a *New York Times* best seller. To date, the novel has been translated into two dozen languages.

Quality: Twenty-five different publications named the novel the best book of the year. Additionally, the book won the Goodreads Readers' Choice Award 2017 in Fiction.

Universal theme: The theme of identity and belonging is poignant in this novel. The narrative sizzles with characters who wish to find a comfortable place in society, and others who believe they set the standards for the American dream.

Imaginative plot: In the book, Celeste details the lives of young people who are quizzical about the concept of poverty. Celeste writes, "Moody almost could not believe that people could be so poor." For example, when Moody's family, the Richardsons, befriends a poor family, Moody experiences how his parents treat disadvantaged people. His parents' behavior, in the new relationship, underscores the Richardson's family values. In a writing style that could be described as plain or even pithy, Celeste spins an elaborate story of two families from opposite sides of the track. Without being superfluous, Celeste gives the readers a complete and intriguing backstory that brings to light hotbed subjects like interracial adoption, socioeconomic status, and personal transformation. As a bonus, Celeste details social interactions and moral decisions that are meant to make her readers uncomfortable.

Lesson plan: Full of controversial topics like abortion, transracial adoption, and obsession, the storylines in this novel could spark heated classroom debates. The obligations the rich have to the poor is the most benign of the topics threaded in this novel.

Talking points: Socioeconomic status (SES) is the totality of a person's wealth, goods, and access to information and social resources. SES plays an important role in the lives of adolescents, their self-perceptions as well as their perceptions of the external world. Celeste offers a novel featuring adolescents that are socializing with clear knowledge of the disparities that exist between the haves and have nots. The juxtaposition of the two social statuses creates a tension that is realistic, albeit uncomfortable. The following are possible discussion questions that could help young readers process the novel.

- Are rich people obligated to share their wealth with poor people? If so, in what ways?
- When does SES become an obstacle in a friendship?
- At what point in your life did you recognize and understand SES?

Standard area CC.1.2.11–12.D: Evaluate how an author's point of view or purpose shapes the content and style of a text: Using a subject from the novel like socioeconomic status or transracial adoption, detail Celeste Ng's point of view on these topics. How does Ng's point of view shape the content and style of the novel?

Vocabulary preview: Before reading the text, the teacher can preview words and concepts like adoption, transracial adoption, socioeconomic status, stigma, commission, and rectify.

RACHEL: A PLAY IN THREE ACTS

The play *Rachel* (London: Oberon, 1916), which depicts an African American family whose members are emotionally affected by racism in 1916, is one that high school students may study.

The expression 'the home is where the heart is' reminds us all that the home is the place where you are safe to be the real and true you. There is nothing more beautiful than unbridled joy protected by the warmth and compassion of the family hearth and home. When carefully tended by the loving arms of the mother, the home becomes a cocoon of comfort and source of self-care. It is the refuge from a storm. What happens, however, when a raging storm pushes itself into the home by way of the mind or broken heart, threatening a family member's mental state?

A play, or theatrical production, is the perfect genre to study the human condition. In the high school curriculum, playwrights like William Shakespeare, Arthur Miller, and Sophocles are headliners. Sometimes overlooked by curriculum writers are African American playwrights like Pulitzer Prize–winning native son Charles Fuller, James IJames, Ozzie Jones, and Angelina Weld Grimké who are not favored in the Western canon.

Angelina Weld Grimké

Angelina was born in Boston, Massachusetts in 1880 to a biracial father and European mother. Both her parents were activists. Archibald was a lawyer and her mother Sarah was an abolitionist. History books note the Grimké sisters as the "only White Southern women who became abolitionists."

When Angelina was very young, her parents' marriage suffered under the weight of oppressive racism since Archibald was considered a Negro by his community. When they split up, Angelina went to live with her mother for a spell. Not too long after, her mother relinquished custody to Archibald and cut all ties with the family. Sadly, the family would learn that Sarah had died by way of suicide.

Quality of writing: In Angelina Weld Grimké's three-act play, the audience is first engulfed by the loving family. The tight-knit family, despite having little monetary means in 1916, offers an abundance of love to Jimmy Mason, a neighborhood boy who needs a haven. Through expertly crafted dialogue and heart-rending soliloquies, the audience experiences the joys and tragedy of being Black in the North.

Universal theme: In her play, Grimké spins a drama that unabashedly depicts a family enjoying each other's love and affection. Rachel, the play's protagonist, is a free-spirited young lady with joy overflowing that can hardly be contained by the elders in her life. Despite her mother's dismay, Rachel's quest to protect the "brown and Black children" in her neighborhood and perhaps the whole world propels Rachel into a downward spiral.

Imaginative plot: Grimké wrote the play, which was promoted by the NAACP as "race propaganda in order to enlighten the American people," to give the public a glimpse into the phenomenon referred to as "Black joy" and its counterpart "Black boy joy."

Lesson plan: "Black joy," a popular subject in Black culture, is permeating mainstream society. Students can learn why this term exists.

Talking points: Loosely defined, "Black joy" is a celebration of African American culture and the art of survival.

- What recent events may have led Black people to create hashtags, videos, and memes about the innate joy that they may feel when loving the Black culture?
- What plays, by African American playwrights, depict Black joy?
- In what ways do you celebrate the Black or African American culture?

Standard areas CC.1.3.11–12.B: Cite strong and thorough textual evidence to support analysis of what the text says explicitly, as well as inferences and conclusions based on and related to an author's implicit and explicit assumptions and beliefs: Choose a theme of the play like Black boy joy or racial trauma and provide textual evidence from the play to support an analysis of Rachel's experiences as well as her implicit and explicit assumptions and beliefs.

Vocabulary preview: Before reading the text, the teacher can preview words and concepts like Black boy joy, racial trauma, and abolitionist.

THE LESSER BLESSED

Richard Van Camp's *The Lesser Blessed* (Vancouver: Douglas & McIntyre, 1996) is a realistic fiction novel depicting a fictional character named Larry Sole.

The onslaught of entertainment products promoted as "young adult" features violence and mature storylines. Few companies that produce young adult entertainment self-censor. The young adult fiction world is no different. Parents and teachers may not like this advertising adage, but it doesn't change the truth: sex sells. Sex sells most merchandise from books to barstools.

Publishing companies are not blind to the advertising frenzy created when controversy piques the collective curiosity. Sex, drugs, and rock and roll, the triad on which pop culture is built, are the most popular controversial subjects in young adult (YA) novels. Although YA novels boldly promote books with controversial subjects like abortion, drugs, police brutality, and mail-order brides, schools do not shy away from including these titles in school and classroom libraries.

Richard Van Camp

Richard was born on September 8, 1971, into the *Dogrib (Tłı̨chǫ)* Nation from Fort Smith, Northwest Territories. He found literary fame with his novel *The Lesser Blessed* which was published in 1996 and adapted into a film directed by Anita Doron in 2012. This literary venture secured Van Camp's spot as the first member of the Dogrib tribe to publish a novel. *Whistle*, published in 2015, is Van Camp's second novel. Van Camp, a graduate of the En'owkin International School of Writing, continued to refine his talents at the University of Victoria's Creative Writing Program and the University of British Columbia's Writing Program where he earned a BFA and a master's degree respectively.

Quality of writing: The critically acclaimed novel *The Lesser Blessed* is a coming-of-age story that details the adventures of Larry Sole, a Dogrib teenager, and Johnny Beck, a suave antagonist who disrupts Larry's world. Johnny and Larry, along with several other teens revel in outrageous shenanigans in the small town of Fort Simmer, a fictional place that mirrors Van Camp's real hometown. The author delights readers with poignant dialogue that is also raw, and blush-worthy at times. Along with the dialogue that includes dialect and idiosyncratic phrases that sting, Van Camp's descriptions of Fort Simmer and the local yokels are visceral, pulling you into a town where the culture of poverty is part of the plot.

Universal theme: Van Camp's novel includes several taboo subjects. Larry Sole, the main character is battling demons, including memories of a horrific accident, when Johnny Beck shows up. Stomping on Larry's turf and flaunting sexual exploits with the girl Johnny is dating (in his head), topics like promiscuous sex, drugs, and parental incest drag the reader to face the prevailing theme: confronting your past is a hard, yet healthy way to heal.

Imaginative plot: Through episodic accounts of Fort Simmer life, and urban legends, Larry and Johnny experience the fast track to adulthood while celebrating the death of innocence. Using a rock and roll soundtrack and salacious slang for readers to delve into, Van Camp shares his culture with his readers.

Lesson plan: Van Camp's novel illustrates how important it is for young people to pay attention to their mental health. The World Health Organization provides helpful information about mental illness and how it plagues the young adult community.

Talking points: The term "coming of age" is used to describe the transition a person experiences when they leave childhood and enter adulthood. In many cultures, this transition is celebrated through various events.

- How does your culture celebrate the transition from childhood to adulthood?
- Do you have a coming-of-age story?
- Why is adolescence such a critical time in a young person's life?

Standard areas CC.1.3.11–12.C: Analyze the impact of the author's choices regarding how to develop and relate elements of a story or drama: Analyze Larry and Johnny's friendship and the sequence of events that led to the main conflict. A student can detail his thoughts of how the plot points helped to create the tension in the book.

Vocabulary preview: Before reading the text, the teacher can preview words and concepts like Indigenous, tribe, incest, and quest.

ANNIE JOHN

Annie John is a coming-of-age novel by Jamaica Kincaid. Kincaid's novels are mostly biographical. This includes her groundbreaking novel *My Brother* (New York: Farrar, Straus and Giroux, 1997), which details the heart wrenching life and death of her baby brother Devon Drew who died from AIDS.

Jamaica Kincaid

Born in St. John's, the Antiguan native author began her life as Elaine Potter Richardson on May 25, 1949. When she was born, her parents did not predict that Elaine would come to be celebrated as the "most important West Indian woman writing today." Kincaid, the author of many notable books, reveals much of her dramatic life in her work.

One of the few Black authors to break into the young adult novel industry, Kincaid's work usually chronicles a character's journey from adolescence to adulthood. *Annie John* displays Kincaid's keen understanding of an adolescent's personal and emotional struggle as Annie tries desperately to burst a bubble of comfort in the effort to become independent.

Universal theme: Often the center of much discussion and analysis, the mother-daughter relationship is a yarn that authors love to spin. Kincaid's novel weaves in nuances like homosexuality and separation anxiety that add to the theme's intrigue. To counteract the tension, Kincaid soothes the soul as the reader is emotionally swaddled by descriptions of the idyllic milieu.

Imaginative plot: The coming-of-age theme is a popular one in literature because the journey from youth to adulthood is a fascinating and often painful time. In the novel, Annie is catapulted into adulthood destroying Annie's relationship with her mother while sparking a raging war within Annie who is grappling with the juxtaposition of her cocoon-like world and that of a cruel one.

Lesson plan: A lesson may center on the lives of young people in the public eye who represent the social, political, or racial turmoil experienced by many teens today.

Talking points: In the book *Annie John* (1984), Kincaid offers a captivating story of a girl and her mother. The relationship, which leaves a lot to be desired, is filled with hostility. Psychologists tell us that the mother-and-daughter relationship is complicated for many reasons.

For the girls:

- Describe your relationship with your mother?
- Is the relationship nurturing or toxic?
- If the relationship is toxic, how can you let your mother know that you are not feeling loved and supported?

For the boys:

- The mother and daughter relationship is often complicated, how can you support your mother as she strengthens her relationship with her daughter?
- How can you support your sister as she works through feelings of angst?

Standard areas CC.1.3.8.C: Analyze how particular lines of dialogue or incidents in a story or drama propel the action, reveal aspects of a character, or provoke a decision: Using the relationship between Annie and her mother, choose lines of dialogue that reveal aspects of their relationship and characterization of the two characters.

Vocabulary preview: Before reading the text, the teacher can preview words and concepts like episodic form, disdain, plaits, spinster, milieu, and colonizers.

ANOTHER BROOKLYN

In *Another Brooklyn* (HarperCollins 2016), Woodson reveals her fandom for Brooklyn.

Jacqueline Woodson

Jacqueline Woodson, a native of Ohio and winner of the Newbery Medal, is no stranger to the coming-of-age story. The author of over a dozen novels, Woodson reveals her penchant for the genre in her novel *Another Brooklyn*, a novel featuring Brooklyn, NY, where Woodson spent much of her childhood.

Now, at fifty-seven years old, Woodson still gives off the air of youth and vitality. Often spotted sporting a leather backpack and signature natural twists, Woodson celebrates the Black experience in many of her books. Her fans are plentiful and eager to collect tidbits about the elusive Woodson.

On her newly updated site Jacquelinewoodson.com, fans can learn that right-handed Woodson can only write with the notebook turned sideways.

On a more personal side, Woodson, an LGBTQ member, struggled with the Jehovah Witness faith her family practiced when she was a child. No longer a practicing member of the religion, Woodson and her partner Juliet Widoff, a physician, reside in Brooklyn.

Quality: Through a cast of characters named August, Sylvia, Gigi, and Angela, and rich descriptions of 1970s Brooklyn, Woodson details the milieu of her old stomping grounds. The fun and drama the inner-city quad experienced through many trials and tribulations makes you wish you were a tag-along turning the clothesline that moonlighted as a double-dutch rope.

Universal theme: Gifted in spinning the coming-of-age tale, Woodson wrote the story in first-person point of view. The characters' feelings are perfectly illustrated through authentic dialogue and stunning imagery that help the reader share the "weight of growing up Girl in Brooklyn" (Woodson, 2016, p. 3). Woodson describes Brooklyn with words that sparkle: "longer nails and sharper blades."

Additionally, the technique of using a personal, down-to-earth tone, helps the book read like a personal journal. Each girl sports her own idiosyncrasy making them a mixed bag of personalities. Angela, with her "high-yellow skin" is a nail-biter who tends to her afro come hell or high water. Gigi whose grandmother came to "South Carolina by way of a Chinaman daddy and mulatto mama" gifted Gigi with eyes of China man and heavy thick braids.

Besides a host of charming and endearing qualities, Woodson stirs the story of each girl with colorful additives of pop or historical references. For example, Woodson gives a nod to the Ibo people, a tribe "someplace off the coast of South Carolina brought over by slave catchers who tossed themselves into the water" believing that "since the water had brought them here, the water would take them home. They believed going home to the water was far better than living their lives enslaved" (Woodson, 2016, p. 167).

Imaginative plot: In this book, August, Sylvia, Gigi, and Angela are teen-age "supergirls" who escape the pitfalls of the inner-city while grappling with the hands of rogue and lascivious men. While facing many daily storms, the four girls dazzle the readers with their lives which are wrapped in jazz music, bell bottoms, afros, and a Southern buffet featuring iconic dishes like chitterlings, pickled pigs' feet, and pork rinds. With tenacious spirits, the young girls fight the world.

Lesson plan: This book is an ideal specimen to teach the literary term "milieu." A term defined as surroundings, especially of a social or cultural nature, milieu is brought to life in *Another Brooklyn*. A teacher can use the book as the platform for student writing the milieu of their own neighborhoods, cities, or towns.

Talking points: Woodson's novel is a great conversation starter for high school students. Listed below are four possible talking points or writing prompts:

- The struggles of inner-city life
- Teenage struggles
- The Black experience in America
- The power of friendship

Standard areas CC.1.4.9–10.A: Write informative/explanatory texts to examine and convey complex ideas, concepts, and information clearly and accurately: Choose a topic from the list and write an informative text that examines an idea from the story.

Vocabulary preview: Before reading the text, the teacher can preview words and concepts like symbolism. Students can describe the symbolic purpose of objects in the novel like the urn of ashes.

DOES MY HEAD LOOK BIG IN THIS?

Randa Abdel-Fattah's first novel *Does My Head Look Big in This?* (Australia: Macmillan, 2005) is a coming-of-age novel.

As we may remember, the teen years are when you strive to be more like others and nothing like yourself. Individuality is social suicide. Instead, teens spend hours flooding social media with selfies that prove they are following the adolescent social order: cloning for acceptance. Occasionally, we hear of a teenager who bucks the system, and goes rogue risking alienation, and perhaps pokes the bear also known as a bully.

Although the yearning to be accepted as an individual despite the magnetic pull to think like the crowd is difficult for boys it is especially hard for girls. Within an hour, girls are bombarded with thousands of images depicting female perfection. Alicia Keys, world renowned singer and songwriter, details her distress with female perfection in her autobiography. In her life, Keys wins the struggle to define herself "in a world that rarely encourages a true and unique identity." Randa Abdel-Fattah's first novel mirrors this concept.

Randa Abdel-Fattah

Born to Palestinian and Egyptian parents in 1979 in Sydney, Australia, Randa began her writing career in her late teens. While studying at the University of Melbourne, she found opportunities to write for various newspapers. It was on that platform that Randa found the courage to hold the media responsible for their representation of Muslims. After completing her undergraduate degree, Randa continued her education, earning a PhD studying Islamophobia and becoming a public speaker on the subject. Her studies of the anti-Muslim sentiment cemented the foundation for her work as an author of award-winning books.

Quality of writing: Abdel-Fattah's book tells the story of Amal Mohamed Nasrullah Abdel-Hakim, a sixteen-year-old Australian Palestinian-Muslim girl who could have easily melted into the social pot without raising any eyebrows. Instead, she upset the applecart when she decides to honor her religion by wearing the hijab, a veil that covers the head and chest, worn by some Muslim women. Afraid that the students at McClean's Preparatory School may reject her, Amal's parents aren't thrilled with the idea. Despite their fears, she wears the hijab, which represents modesty, to school. Abdel-Fattah's use of natural dialogue brings to life realistic characters who spit in the face of Amal's religious bravery.

Universal theme: Despite parental dismay and Islamophobia, Amal prevails in achieving self-expression and religious freedom, recalling strong-willed women like Brooklyn native Linda Sarsour, who was named one of *Time* magazine's "100 Most Influential People" in 2017.

Imaginative plot: In writing the novel, Abdel-Fattah hoped to give her readers a story that "debunked the common misconceptions about Muslims which allowed readers to enter the world of the average Muslim teenage girl and see past the headlines and stereotypes," Abdel-Fattah says.

Lesson plan: Islamophobia, an exaggerated and illogical fear of Muslims which may incite a person to show aggression toward Muslims, is on the rise in the United States. Students can learn why this fear has increased since the September 11 attacks in 2001 (also referred to as 9/11).

Talking points:

• What are some of the most significant instances of Islamophobia attacks that occurred in the United States?
• If a person said "all Muslims are terrorists" in your presence, how would you respond?
• Do you think Muslims condemn terrorism?

Standard areas CC.1.4.9–10.A: Write informative/explanatory texts to examine and convey complex ideas, concepts, and information clearly and accurately: Choose a topic from the list and write an informative text that examines your thoughts on the topic.

Vocabulary preview: Before reading the text, the teacher can preview words and concepts like Muslim, Islamophobia, pious, agnostic, and hijab.

THE LIFE OF A GIRL WHO USES A WHEELCHAIR

Published in 1981, *Alesia*, by Eloise Greenfield and Alesia Revis, details the struggles a young African American girl who became physically disabled as the result of being hit by a car. There are few fiction books that include characters with disabilities and less that include people of color with disabilities.

Eloise Greenfield

Born May 17, 1929, in North Carolina, Eloise moved to Washington, DC, when she was very little. Growing up, one of five children, in Washington, DC, Eloise took an interest in piano and reading. She didn't find her passion for writing until she was in her late twenties. Her goal was to highlight African American culture in her writing. Married with two children and working as a clerk-typist at the US Patent Office, Eloise carved out time to enjoy her passion of writing. She wrote everything including poetry and songs.

Eloise's writing was recognized by many notable writers earning her the Recognition of Merit Award in 1990. The award was presented by the George G. Stone Center for Children's Books in Claremont, California. Eloise also received an honorary degree from Wheelock College in Boston, MA. Although Eloise is a prolific writer, she never strayed from her main goal: to uplift the African American community through service. With that goal in mind, Eloise used her talents to provide free creative writing workshops to young people with the help of grants from the D.C. Commission on the Arts and Humanities.

Quality of writing: *Alesia* is written as a diary with the character detailing her life as a typical teen who happens to be physically handicapped. The diary entries are easy-going accounts of teen life with snippets of how Alesia's disability affects her day-to-day existence.

Universal theme: We read her entries and realize that the Spring of 1980 was bursting full of fun stuff like school dances, family gatherings, and trips to McDonald's. Alesia's diary entries are not disheartening stories about how her physical disability disables her. Instead, Alesia details how her life with a wheelchair has a few pitfalls. Alesia writes how she meets those pitfalls and challenges with grit, determination, courage, and humor.

Imaginative plot: This book represents inclusive literature that "reflects the diversity of children's life experiences." Alesia lives a life in this book that may help young people feel included.

Lesson plan: Writers can support inclusivity by creating characters with or without disabilities who share the gamut of experiences and emotions that humans encounter.

Talking points:

- What fiction books have you read that depict disabled people?
- In your opinion, why are people with mental or physical disabilities often left out of fiction?
- According to research, there are 5.8 million physically disabled children in America. What are some ways readers can demand that disabled people are properly and accurately represented in literature?

Standards areas CC.1.4.8.I: Acknowledge and distinguish the claim(s) from alternate or opposing claims and support claim with logical reasoning and relevant evidence, using accurate, credible sources and demonstrating an understanding of the topic: Think about the ways your neighborhood can consider the needs of physically disabled people. Write an essay that begins with a claim regarding the changes people need to make to accommodate the disabled.

Websites preview: Before reading the text, the teacher can preview, with the students, various websites dedicated to information regarding physical disabilities.

CONCLUSION

Book recommendations are invitations to a well-planned library. Using personalized details gleaned from the reading survey, a teacher can increase reading motivation by providing students with reading freedom. With attention to questions and details that can stimulate a student's frame of reference, the Reading QUILT Book Reviews are recommendations that highlight young adult literature and promote reader engagement.

Realistic fiction has done much to popularize YA fiction offering provocative topics that may peak a student's interests. While it is fun to see students get excited about reading, teachers must be well-equipped to guide students in subject areas that are considered sensitive. Multicultural literature, which includes selections in every genre, is ideal for pushing the boundaries of the typical literature that is commonly available to students.

Using book recommendations, teachers can provide students with alternatives to the White, middle-class, cisgender, and heterosexual lifestyles that have become the traditional and accepted stories of America. Instead, these multicultural selections represent coming-of-age stories and other themes featuring protagonists of color who invite readers to have vicarious cultural experiences. Additionally, the recommendations, aligned with state academic standards, are ideal for lesson planning.

Appendix A

The Research Project

In 2019, the author conducted a research project to survey the body of multicultural literature included in eighth grade summer reading lists of ten northeastern, suburban, private middle schools, near a bustling metropolitan city, to determine if the assigned fiction books promote a multicultural curriculum.

Rooted in the work of Paulo Freire (1974), which informs critical multiculturalism, the research included in the study is meant to bring awareness to the prevalent idea that racism and cultural pluralism are still problems in America while challenging the systemic obstacles that impede the adoption of a multicultural curriculum.

Research shows that the US standard curriculum is racially biased and lacking in stories that detail the struggles as well as the intellectual, social, political, and cultural contributions and pursuits of racialized and underrepresented people. In conducting this qualitative content analysis, the author suggests that quality multicultural literature can foster racial tolerance and alleviate racial tension among students. Furthermore, teachers who lack the avidity to embrace multicultural literature pose a significant problem in education.

RESEARCH DESIGN AND QUESTIONS

The author used content analysis to name and code categorical distinctions related to the term "multicultural" provided by Sleeter and Grant (1988) such as author's authority, gender, sexual orientation, racial description, physical handicap, and socioeconomic status. Additionally, the author also explored each book's use of literary elements like dialect, point of view, setting, imagery, word choice, and universal themes (see figure A.1). Overall,

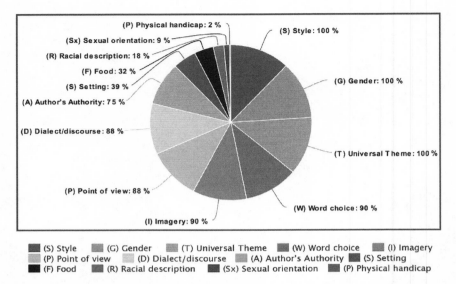

(S) Style   **(G) Gender**   **(T) Universal Theme**   **(W) Word choice**   **(I) Imagery**
(P) Point of view   **(D) Dialect/discourse**   **(A) Author's Authority**   **(S) Setting**
(F) Food   **(R) Racial description**   **(Sx) Sexual orientation**   **(P) Physical handicap**

Figure A.1   The Percentages of Each Code Represented in the Study. *Created by the author*

content analysis helped the author recognize patterns of information from the frequency of words or phrases found in each novel.

The content analysis was used to answer the following research questions: (1) What percentage of summer reading books fit the category of multicultural literature that the literature "recognizes, accepts, and affirms human differences and similarities related to gender, race, handicap, and class" (Sleeter and Grant, 1988)? (2) Do the summer books include universal themes that present multiple dimensions of a culture objectively and without bias? (3) What are the demographics of the people selecting the summer reading books?

To answer the research questions, the author collected data from a sample of 43 summer reading books obtained from a population of 144 fiction books.

RESULTS

The first research question asked: What percentage of summer reading books fit the category of "multicultural literature," in that the literature "recognizes, accepts, and affirms human differences and similarities related to gender, race, handicap, and class"? The data to answer this research question is as follows:

- (A) Author's authority: 75 percent of the authors shared the same background as the protagonist.
- (G) Gender: 100 percent of the authors described characters in the "female/feminine" and "male/masculine" pronouns.
- (Sx) Sexual orientation: 9 percent of the authors described protagonists as having a sexual identity of either homosexual or bisexual.
- (R) Racial description: 18 percent the authors wrote physical descriptions of their characters' ethnic traits.
- (H) Physical handicap: 2 percent of the authors described their protagonists as being physically or mentally impaired.
- (Se) Socioeconomic status: 100 percent the authors included details in the book that alluded to their protagonists' social and economic factors that defined their financial, social, and cultural capital.

The second research question asked: Do summer reading books include universal themes that present multiple dimensions of a culture objectively and without bias? This study's findings show that 100 percent of the novels featured universal themes without bias. The most frequently occurring universal themes were racism, self-discovery, and courage. The least frequently found themes were the American dream, peaceful coexistence, and adventure (see figure A.2).

The third research question asked: What are the demographics of the people selecting summer reading literature choices? What methods do the

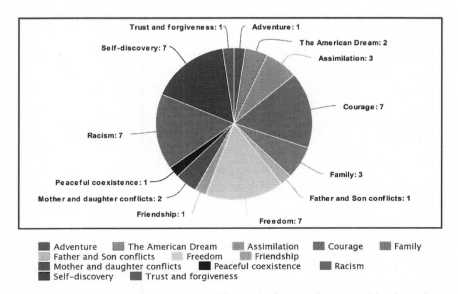

Figure A.2 The Percentage of Universal Themes in the Sample. *Created by the author*

teachers and administrators use to choose the books? The author sent a survey via email to each teacher or administrator who had the charge of compiling each school's summer reading list. On the survey, 100 percent of the administrators identified as White. Specifically, 80 percent of the administrators identified as White females, and 20 percent as White males. Additionally, teachers and administrators use sources like Bookrags.com, Amazon.com, and Publishers Weekly to select books that are described as multicultural.

IMPLICATIONS FOR EDUCATORS

The modern US curriculum, which is based in a large part on the New England classical liberal curriculum, is Eurocentric, heavy, and deleterious to students of color since it promotes feelings of loneliness and powerlessness. Keeping the mental state of students in mind, how can school stakeholders amend the standard curriculum although it does not provide the opportunity for quick changes? Curriculum administrators can supplement the curriculum with summer reading that celebrates diversity through a selection of multicultural books and corresponding materials.

A move to integrate multicultural literature in the curriculum is desperately needed. Despite the increasing diversity in American classrooms, students are not offered narratives that foster "meaningful encounters with others living in the US who are different from themselves" (Moya and Hamedani, 2017, 10). Students living in racial disharmony and racial unrest are impatiently waiting for a change.

Appendix B
Charts and Definitions

Diversity in Schools and Publishing

Student diversity in US public schools 2017–2018	Teaching population 2017–2018	Diversity in publishing 2019
13.6 million Hispanic, Latino, and Mexican students were enrolled in the US public school system.	Hispanic, Latino, and Mexican teachers made up 9 percent of the US public school teaching population.	Hispanic, Latino, and Mexican people made up 6 percent of the publishing industry (not the executive positions).
2.8 million Asian, Pacific Islander, and Native Hawaiian students were enrolled in the US public school system.	Asian, Pacific Islander, and Native Hawaiian teachers made up less than 1 percent of the US public school teaching population.	Asian, Pacific Islander, and Native Hawaiian people made up 7 percent of the publishing industry (not the executive positions).
7.7 million Black and African American students were enrolled in the US public school system.	Black and African American teachers made up 7 percent of the US public school teaching population.	Black and African American people made up 5 percent of the publishing industry (not the executive positions).

Terms, Definitions, and Abbreviations Used in Evaluating Multicultural Literature

Terms	Definitions	Abbreviations
Author authenticity	Author's formal, background, or firsthand knowledge (Wilfong 2007).	A
Gender identity	The physical state of being male or female. The person's perception of having a particular gender, which may or may not correspond with their birth sex (VandenBos 2015).	G
Sexual orientation	A person's sexual identity in relation to the gender to which they are attracted; the fact of being heterosexual, homosexual, or bisexual (VandenBos 2015).	Sx
Race and ethnicity	A person's self-identification with one or more social groups. Relating to races or large groups of people who have the same customs, religion, or origin (Humes and Jones 2011).	R
Handicap (physical)	Physical disabilities are impairments which limit an individual's physical function (Mitchell 2017, vii).	H
Socioeconomic status	The interaction of social and economic factors which can include human, financial, social, and cultural capital (Perkins 2016, 2).	Se
Dialect and discourse	The vernacular, slang, or language pattern that is particular or peculiar to a specific region or social group (Smith, Echols, Bryant, Howell, and Ming 2004).	D
Point of view (characters)	The protagonist's and support characters' points of view, opinions, or their angle of considering things (Mathonsi and Canonici, 2009).	POV
Setting	The primary setting is natural in relation to the content of the book and described without using stereotypes. Additionally, the researcher noted if the setting is universal instead of "typical" to the culture in a stereotypical way (MerriamWebster.com).	S
Style	Within this theme coded as "ST," the researcher observed if the novel's content is easily understood by both members of the culture portrayed and other readers. Style describes the ways that the author uses words, sentence structure, figurative language, and sentence arrangement (Read. Write. Think. 2013).	St
Word choice	Part of a writer's style includes his choice of words to help the reader conjure up certain images (literarydevices.net).	W
Universal Theme	The theme should be universal and apply to all cultures (Shea 2010, 35).	T
Food	The author includes food that connects or relates to the protagonist's culture or setting. The author can use food as a subtheme in a book.	F

Curated Multicultural Book Lists

List of Curators and Founders	List of Subjects	Website	Year Published
Curator: Gerald Moore, Charleston County Library branch manager	African American literature	https://www.ccpl.org/branches	2020
Founder: Sarah Mangiola	Multicultural literature	Readbrightly.com	2020
Founder: Katie Cunningham	Award-winning books remind young readers they belong	theclassroombookshelf.com	2020
Founders: Janeice and Reginald Haynes	Multicultural literature	detroitbookcity.com	2020
Founder: Alli Harper	The best of children's books featuring diverse characters	ourshelves.com	2020
Curators: Anastasia Collins, Cynthia Bolin, Krista Aronson, Megan Dowd Lambert, and Rianna Matthews-Brown			
Founders: Carolyn Danckaert and Aaron Smith	Mighty girls	amightygirl.com	2020
We Need Diverse Books editors	Features "a wide array of titles with diverse content and by creators from marginalized communities."	diversebooks.org/ourstory	2020
Founder: D'Juan Hopewell	5 Black chefs with cookbooks	webuyblack.com	2020
Founders: Wade Hudson and Cheryl Willis Hudson	"Positive, vibrant Black-interest books,"	justusbooks.com	1987–present
Founders: Valarie Budayr and Mia Wenjen	Read your world: diverse books	https://multiculturalchildrens bookday.com/	2020
Curator: Karen Cicero	44 children's books about mental health	childmind.org	2020
Curators: Reading Rockets' staff	Children's books featuring characters with autism and Asperger's	readingrockets.org	2020
Founder: Kelly Starling Lyons	The Brown Bookshelf	thebrownbookshelf.com	2020
Founder: Tonya Alexander	Books Exposed	Booksexposed.com	2014

(Continued)

Curated Multicultural Book Lists (*Continued*)

List of Curators and Founders	List of Subjects	Website	Year Published
Founder: Corinne Sullivan	100 plus books by Black women that should be essential for everyone	popsugar.com	2020
Curator: Caroline Bologna	17 children's books that promote understanding of autism	huffpost.com	2018
Founder: Cameron Esposito	5 books for a queer road trip	lithub.com	2020
Founder: L. Simn	10 LGBTQ books recommended by librarians	ilovelibraries.org	2020
Founder: The Rumpus	What to read when you want to celebrate women's history month	therumpus.net	2020
Founder: Jasamine Hill	4 personal development books written for and by Black women	xonecole.com	2020
Curator: Amanda Morris	Teach about Native American women leaders	tolerance.org	2018
Founder: Aliyah Chavez	Empower Native kids to read	indiancountrytoday.com	2020
Curators: Social Justice Books editors	Women's history month: a book everyday	socialjusticebooks.og	2020
Founder: Charlotte Riggle	14 picture books with disabled characters	charlotteriggle.com	2018
Founder: Christina Douglas-Williams	Black books are for White children too	bebombbookclub.com	2020
Curator: Pooja Makhijani	10 books with South Asian characters you should read in 2020	teenvogue.com	2020
Founder: Alejandra Oliva	15 books by Latino and Latin American authors to add to your 2020 reading list	remezcla.com	2020
Curator: Guest blogger	The importance of Black science fiction and why every black person should read genre	blackgirlnerds.com	2020

Founder: Ashia Ajani	8 Black eco-poets who inspire us	sierraclub.org	2020
Curator: Siobhan Neela-Stok	7 new children's and young adult books to read for Black history month and beyond	mashable.com	2020
Curator: Laura Sackton	20 must-read audiobooks narrated by black women	bookriot.com	2020
Curators: Ehis Osifo, Farrah Penn	31 YA books by black authors that you can't miss this year	buzzfeed.com	2019
Curator: S. E. Fleenor	13 nonbinary writers and comic creators changing science fiction and fantasy	syfy.com	2020
Curator: Samantha McIntyre	The best children's books to celebrate black history month	parenting.com	2020
Curators: Successful Black Parenting, editors	Black children's books you don't know about yet!	successfulblackparenting.com	2019
Curators: The Master Playbook	Personal finance books by African American authors	themasterplaybook.com	2020
Olivia Mason and Kelsey McConnell	Black science fiction and fantasy authors you need to read	theportalist.com	2020
Because of them We Can staff	29 Black authors to support during black history month	becauseofthemwecan.com	2020
Sadeqa Johnson	8 books featuring memorable African American characters	booktrib.com	2020
Black Parent Team	Black history month celebrated every day with these middle grade books	blackparentmagazine.com	2018
K. W. Colyard	18 new books about the immigrant experience that aren't *American Dirt*	bustle.com	2020

(Continued)

Curated Multicultural Book Lists (*Continued*)

List of Curators and Founders	List of Subjects	Website	Year Published
Tom Berger	22 diverse book choices for all grade levels	edutopia.org	2019
Erika T. Wurth	14 contemporary books by Native American writers to get excited about	buzzfeednews.com	2020
Scott Woods	28 more black picture books that aren't about boycotts, buses or basketball	Scottwoodmakeslists. wordpress.com	2019
Books for Littles' editors	Don't yuck my yum: kids' books that dismantle orientalism and food shaming	booksforlittles.com	2019
Victoria L. Valentine	Culture type picks: 14 Black art books of 2019	culturetype.com	2020
Ross Johnson	11 works of trans-positive science fiction and fantasy	Barnesandnoble.com	2018
Black baby books' editors	Discover children's books with black characters	blackbabybooks.com	2020
Here Wee Read editors	The best 45 diverse children's books of 2019 to read over and over again	hereweeread.com	2019
Editors at the Conscious Kid Library	Black Books Matter	theconsciouskid.org	2016

Texts in the Canon and Alternative Texts

Universal Themes	Multicultural Text	Canon Selections	Grade Level
The coexistence of good and evil racism	Reynolds & Kiely 2015. *All American Boys*. Delran: Simon and Schuster.	*To Kill a Mockingbird* by Harper Lee	Upper School
The inevitability of fate	Abdel-Fattah, R. 2007. *Does My Head Look Big in This?* New York: Orchard Books.	*Romeo and Juliet* by William Shakespeare	Middle School
The individual versus society			
The phoniness of the adult world	Quinonez, E. 2000. *Bodega Dreams*. New York: Vintage Contemporaries.	*The Catcher in the Rye* by J.D. Salinger	Upper School
Self-discovery			
Crossing boundaries	Thomas, A. 2017. *The Hate U Give* (Unabridged). New York: Balzer + Bray.	*Frankenstein* by Mary Shelley	Upper School
Revenge			
Powerlessness	Myers, W. 1999. *Monster*. New York: Harper Collins Publishing.	*Of Mice and Men* by John Steinbeck	Upper School
Freedom/confinement			
Slavery	Kidd, S. M. 2014. *The Invention of Wings*. New York: Viking.	*The Adventures of Huckleberry Finn* by Mark Twain	Upper School
Racism			
Love	Kincaid, J. 1997. *Annie John*. New York: Farrar, Straus, and Giroux.	*The Diary of a Young Girl* by Anne Frank	Middle School
The mother figure	Angelou, Maya. 2008. *Letter to My Daughter*. New York: Random House.	*Sophie's Choice* by William Styron	Upper School
Sexuality and power			
Emotional burdens	Woodson, J. 2016. *Another Brooklyn: A Novel*. New York: Amistad, an imprint of HarperCollins Publishers.	*The Things They Carried* by Tim O'Brien	Upper School
Friendship			
Family	Taylor, Mildred. 1991. *Let the Circle Be Unbroken*. London: Penguin Books.	*Little Women* by Louisa May Alcott	Middle School
Love			

Recommended Multicultural Books for Grades 9–12

Book Title	Author's Ethnicity	Protagonist(s)' Ethnicity	Universal Theme
All American Boys— Grades 11–12	Caucasian/African American (2 authors)	African American/Caucasian	Racism
Amos Fortune— Grades 11–12	Caucasian	African American	Freedom
Annie John— Grades 9–12	Antiguan	Antiguan	Mother/daughter relationships
Autobiography of Miss Jane Pitman— Grades 9–12	African American	African American	Freedom
Behind the Mountains— Grades 7–12	Haitian American	Haitian American	Self-discovery
Bodega Dreams— Grades 9–12	Spanish American	Spanish American	Self-discovery
Brown Girl Dreaming— Grades 7–12	African American	African American	Self-discovery
Buddha in the Attic— Grade 12	Japanese American	Japanese American	Freedom
Call It Courage— Grades 6–8	Caucasian	Caucasian	Courage
Codetalkers— Grades 6–8	Caucasian (Native American ancestry)	Caucasian (Native American ancestry)	Courage
The Crossover— Grades 4–8	African American	African American	Father/son relationship
Cry the Beloved Country— Grades 9–12	South African	South African	Racism
Diamond in the Desert— Grades 4–8	Caucasian	Japanese	Courage
Does My Head Look Big in This?— Grades 7–9	Palestinian Muslim	Palestinian Muslim	Courage

Title—Grade			Theme
The Ear, the Eye, and the Arm—Grades 7–9	Caucasian	South African	Racism
Fiela's Child—Grades 9–12	South African (White)	South African (Black)	Racism
Flygirl—Grades 6–8	African American	African American	Courage
Funny Boy—Grades 9–12	Indian (Sri Lankan)	Indian (Sri Lankan)	Self-discovery
Giovanni's Room—Grade 12	African American	African American	Trust/forgiveness
The Hate You Give—Grades 11–12	African American	African American	Racism
Inside Out and Back Again—Grade 9	Vietnamese	Vietnamese	Courage
The Invention of Wings—Grade 12	Caucasian	Caucasian and African American (2 protagonists)	Friendship
The Journey to America—Grades 6–8	German American	German	Freedom
The Joy Luck Club—Grade 12	Chinese American	Chinese American	Mother/daughter relationships
Let the Circle Be Unbroken—Grade 9	African American	African American	Racism
A Letter to My Daughter—Grades 10–12	African American	African American	Mother/daughter relationships
Mismatch—Grade 9	Chinese American	Chinese American	Assimilation
My Name Is Not Easy—Grades 9–12	Caucasian	Indigenous Alaskan (Inupiaq)	Assimilation
The Revolution of Evelyn Serrano—Grade 9	Puerto Rican American	Puerto Rican American	Self-discovery

(Continued)

Recommended Multicultural Books for Grades 9–12 (Continued)

Book Title	Author's Ethnicity	Protagonist(s)' Ethnicity	Universal Theme
Shadowshaper— Grades 11–12	Afro Puerto Rican (Afro Boricua)	Afro Puerto Rican (Afro Boricua)	Self-discovery
The Skin I'm In— Grade 9	African American	African American	Self-discovery
Somewhere in the Darkness— Grade 9	African American	African American	Father/son relationships

A Page from the Reader's Journal for the Book *Does My Head Look Big in This?*

Book Information	Abbreviations and Descriptions	Examples of Elements
Does My Head Look Big in This? Author: Randa Abdel-Fattah Publisher: Macmillan Publishers, Date published: 2005 Page count: 348	A- Author's Authority: Cultural/ ethnic background	**Author-** Palestinian Muslim; **Protagonist-** Palestinian Muslim
	D- Dialect/discourse of culture (colloquialism/slang) is natural to the culture presented.	Comments Amal hears in school: "Hey, Amal, why does a sneeze sound like a letter in the Arabic language?" (p. 5)
	R- How the race or cultural group is physically described.	"My name is Amal Mohamed Nasrullah Abdel-Hakim. The teachers labeled me slow in preschool because I was the last child to learn how to spell her name" (p. 1).
	G- The physical state of being male or female. The researcher focused mainly on person's perception of having a particular gender, which may or may not correspond with their birth sex.	Amal identifies as a girl using pronouns like "her."
	Sx- A person's sexual identity in relation to the gender to which they are attracted: the fact of being heterosexual, homosexual, or bisexual.	Amal identifies as heterosexual who is attracted to males. "I want to be with one person in my life. I want to know that the guy I spend the rest of my life with is the first person I share something so intimate and exciting with" (p. 15).
	Se- The interaction of social and economic factors.	"We live in Camberwell, one of Melbourne's trendy suburbs, beautiful tree-lined streets, Federation homes, manicured front lawns" (p. 5).

A Page from the Reader's Journal for the book *Buddha in the Attic*

Book Information	Codes and Descriptions	Examples of Codes
Buddha in the Attic, Published by Alfred Knopf; Date published: 2011 129 pages	A- Author's authority: Cultural/ethnic background	**Author:** Japanese **Protagonist:** Japanese
	D- Dialect/discourse of culture (colloquialism/ slang) is natural to the culture presented.	1. The virgins said to each other, "Remind me again. I am Mrs. who?" (p. 5). 2. Mothers taught them, "A girl must blend into a room: she must be present without appearing to exist" (p. 6). 3. The mail-order brides' dream of a new lives (p. 5). 4. Most of us were accomplished and believed we would make good wives (p. 6).
	R- How the race or cultural group is physically described.	The description of Japanese virgins: long black hair, and flat wide feet (p. 3). The various people and cultures the women saw on the boat are described as turbaned Sikhs and the Punjabs fleeing the Panama, sunburned Germans (p. 13).
	G- The physical state of being male or female. The researcher focused mainly on person's perception of having a particular gender, which may or may not correspond with their birth sex.	The girls were described in heterosexual terms using pronouns like she and her. "Some of the girls were natural brooders, stayed to themselves" (p. 15).
	Sx- A person's sexual identity in relation to the gender to which they are attracted; the fact of being heterosexual, homosexual, or bisexual.	The girls were described in terms of pursuing heterosexual sex. "Lots of girl talk at night, romance among the girls, good practice for their husbands anyway" (p. 17).

A Page from the Reader's Journal for the book *Buddha in the Attic* (Continued)

Book Information	Codes and Descriptions	Examples of Codes
	Se- The interaction of social and economic factors.	1. The children did many chores: they hauled water, they cleared brush, they hoed in the blazing summer heat of the Imperial Valley before their bones were fully formed" (p. 64).
		2. Eating on the boat: We ate the same food every day (p. 12).
		3. Description of the deplorable California labor camps where the women worked (p. 23).
		4. The Fair Ranch in Yolo, where some of the wives lived is described as: flea ridden mattresses, dirty old chicken coops, dry beds of hay (p. 24).
Word choice	Part of a writer's style includes his choice of words to help the reader conjure up certain images.	1. Had hair in the appropriate places (p. 7).
		2. The man's brown hair which made the girls shiver (p. 14).
		3. The men admired us for our strong backs and nimble hands (p. 2).

The Reading Survey

Name:_____ Date:_____

Question	Purpose	Activity
What is the history of your name? Did you have a childhood nickname?	Names are personal and often connect to family history.	Name acrostics Research the etymology of your name
Name three of your favorite toys or books from childhood?	Childhood toys and books are sources of fun or fond memories. Children's books may include story themes that can be found in young adult books.	Who invented the toys? Do any of the childhood toys have cultural relevance? Read your favorite childhood books to the class. Write a children's book.
What are your favorite hobbies? Do you have talents that you would like to share with the community?	Hobbies and talents are sources of pride.	Share the talent with the class in person or as a video.
What are you passionate about? What profession are you planning to have in the future?	Students enjoy talking about their passions.	Research the people of color who worked in your profession.
Do you enjoy writing? Do you have writing you would like to share with the community?	A student's personal writing can be used as a platform for formal writing.	Using your writing, create a blog, book, or mixed media art.
What type of entertainment do you like? What is your favorite movie, television show, music, musical group, and song? What is your favorite commercial?	Movies and television shows can indicate the type of humor a student enjoys. Additionally, the entertainment or music may be culturally relevant. Commercials can illustrate a specific interest.	Share your music or a clip of your favorite show with your class.
Do you have a pet?	Pets are often considered family members.	Share pictures of your pet with your class. Describe how the pet became a part of your life.

(Continued)

The Reading Survey (*Continued*)

Name:_____   Date:_____

Question	Purpose	Activity
Do you enjoy reading? What subjects or ideas do you like to read about? In what form do you like your reading sources? Digital articles, hardcopy books, social media messages, online magazines, blogs? Do you have a favorite author or genre? Do you have a favorite book? Describe your reading time? What is the best way for you to read? Silent, aloud, in bed, on the couch?	There are a variety of reading sources available to students.	Make a list of the sources where you get your reading material. Share excerpts of your favorite reading with the class.
If you were going to write a book, what would be the plot? Do you think your life would make a good movie or biopic? Why or why not?	A student who does not enjoy reading may say that there aren't any books written about what he likes. The answer to this question may help a teacher find books for the student.	Create a cast list of your movie or biopic using famous actors.
What personal traits do your friends appreciate about you? What personality traits rub you the wrong way?	These questions may help the teacher identify personality traits that a student does or does not appreciate.	Name a television show that features a character you like or don't like. Explain why.
Do you have any memes you would like to share with the class?	Often students gravitate to memes that are culturally or personally relevant.	Create a vision board that includes your memes.
What do you hope your teacher learns about you, your culture, and your life?	This question helps the student provide additional details.	Using a copy of a page from a favorite book, create a found poem. Using the "I Am From" template, create a poem about yourself.

At the start of the school year, students can work on the survey just a few minutes each class period. The questions are designed to gather information that may help a teacher find books the student may enjoy. The survey provides insight on how each question is helpful in relationship building as well as an activity that allows for creativity. Additionally, a teacher may want to make a mental note of his connections to the student.

Table B.1   Sample Data Collection Chart for Selected Multicultural Books

Title of Book	Author's Cultural Identity	Protagonist's Cultural Identity	Year Published	Theme

APPENDIX B: TEXTBOX 1

Reflection Questions

Reflection questions: These questions are designed to help a teacher consider their hidden biases. For the best results, the teacher can answer the questions in a journal. The journal allows the teacher to elaborate on the answers with details and examples. However, the most effective exploration is done with a partner who can use the reflection questions in an interview-style conversation while prompting the teacher to elaborate without fear of judgment. The first few questions include examples of detailed answers. These examples are included to encourage the teacher to be as detailed as possible for the purpose of exploring their feelings and associations, which may reveal unconscious bias.

Formative years:

- Describe the people in the neighborhoods where you spent most of your time? I spent my entire kindergarten through high school years in a multicultural neighborhood. The neighbors to the left and right of my house were Black. However, across the street from our house lived several White families and one Armenian family. My family maintained friendly relationships with our neighbors. My brother was best friends with one of the White families who had a boy of his age. I was best friends with the boy's sister. Our friends spent lots of afternoons playing in our family room or in our yard.
- When you were young, what warnings, if any, did your parents give you about people in your neighborhood? My parents were very protective of the girls in the family. We played mostly on the porch and in the yard.

Sometimes I walked a few lawns away from my house, which took me to the corner. My mother warned me not to talk to strangers, but she didn't describe them using any racial descriptors.

- What was the racial demographics of each school you attended from elementary through high school? From first through eighth grade, I attended a Catholic school where I was one of ten Black students. Several of the students were Greek. The total population was less than 200 students. In high school, I attended a Catholic girls' school where I was one of five Black students in my freshman class. The total number of minority students was less than 50 in a school of 550 students.
- Describe the ethnic background of your five close friends from your formative years. What warnings did your parents give you about your friends? In elementary school, few kids played with me. Since the students were White, they ostracized me because I looked different than they did. I was often teased about my hair, and skin color. However, I became best friends with a Black girl who enrolled in our school in the fifth grade. It was around the same time when several White girls wanted to become better friends with me. I spent some days hanging out with my Black friend. When I was not with her, I spent time with my White friends. In high school, my close friends and I entered the same high school. We continued to socialize together. My parents did not allow me to go to my friends' houses until I was in high school. I remember my mother warning me not to share combs, brushes, or lip gloss with girls for fear of lice or Mononucleosis.
- Describe the ethnicity of the teachers you had in your formative years.
- How do you think the schools you attended or the relationships you made during your formative years helped inform your feelings about certain racial groups?
- When you were young, what physical qualities did you find beautiful?
- Were you bullied as a child? Describe the people who bullied you?

College years:

- Describe the ethnic demographics of the college you attended?
- Describe the ethnic background of your five close friends from your college years. What warnings did your parents give you about your college friends?
- Describe the ethnicity of the professors you had?
- How do you think the college you attended or the relationships you made during your college years helped inform your feelings about certain racial groups?
- Did you enroll in any classes that taught you about race?

- Did you attend a predominately White college? Why or why not? Did you attend a historically Black college? Why or why not?
- While in college, did you experience social problems? Explain.
- Were you bullied in college? Describe the people who bullied you?

Adult years:

- How do you obtain friends? What limitations do you put on yourself regarding finding, maintaining friend relationships? If you have no or few friends from other cultural backgrounds, explain why this is the case?
- Do you categorize your friends or label the friend using ethnic or cultural terms? For example, do you use the term "my gay friend"?
- Do you take or create opportunities to socialize with people outside of your ethnic or cultural group? Why or why not?
- Where do you socialize with your friends? Are the settings normally monocultural?
- Describe the type of biases you are aware that you possess? Did your formative or college years play a part in the formation of these biases? If so, how?
- Do you have a close friend of a different cultural background than your own with whom you can discuss issues about race, culture, or social justice? How did this friendship start? Why is the friendship important to you?
- Do you use pejorative terms to describe certain houses in our outside of your neighborhood? For example, do you refer to houses as "crack house"? Why or why not? Do you use the term "going slumming"? Why or why not?
- Do you enjoy "off color" jokes when in the presence of friends of your same cultural background?
- Do you believe that people of other cultures treat you poorly? Explain the situation.
- In your college career, did you take any courses in race, race relations, multiculturalism, or multicultural literature? If so, detail your experiences in those courses. What were the demographics of each class?

Professional life:

- Would you use any of these terms to describe yourself? Explain why you choose each term? Ally, anti-racist, or woke.
- Do you teach at a predominately White institution? If so, describe the reasons why.

- What are the racial demographics of the school where you teach or work?
- Describe the ethnicity of the students with whom you have friendly connections and/or are excited to teach.
- Describe the ethnicity of the students who seem to push your buttons or trigger negative responses in you.
- Do you have difficulty making a personal connection with Black male students?
- Describe the ethnicity of the students whom you seem to give "passes" to with the idea that the student is "good for it." Which students do you give leeway or the benefit of the doubt?
- Describe the ethnicity of the students to whom you give leadership roles?
- Describe the ethnicity of the coworkers with whom you socialize with during or after school hours.
- Describe the ethnicity of the coworkers who seem to push your buttons or trigger negative responses in you.
- In general, do you think of people of color as less fortunate than you?
- Are you aware of any microaggressions or racist language that you have committed or spoken? Who made you aware of these microaggressions or comments? How did you respond to the person who brought the information to your attention?
- Are you excessively nice to students who are culturally different than you? If so, explain why?
- What are your musical preferences? Describe your top ten favorite musical groups. When do you listen to music outside of your preferences?
- What are your reading preferences? Describe your top five authors.
- How do you feel about the "Black Lives Matter" movement?
- Do you seek out people of your same cultural background to share good news? Why?
- Do you seek out people of your same cultural background to gossip about a person of a different cultural background? Why?

DEFINITION OF TERMS

Ally eyes: A person who identifies as a White ally will look at systems to see how racism impacts those systems.

Author authority: The firsthand knowledge the author has about the subject or ethnic culture described in the book.

Background knowledge: Essential information associated with the text or idea that helps the reader understand the expressed concepts.

Black joy: A Black person's expression of happiness or exuberance for the Black or African American culture. When shown by a male, this expression is called Black boy joy.

Black Lives Matter Movement: A decentralized social movement whose members advocate for racial tolerance and rally against racially motivated police brutality.

Black Pride: A movement to celebrate Black culture in the face of racism.

Brown vs. the Board of Education: The landmark case that officially ended racial segregation in public schools by deeming racial segregation as unconstitutional.

Coding: In qualitative research, coding is the process of labeling ideas or textual passages for the purpose of categorizing data or finding relationships among data.

Colorblind ideology: Also named "colorblindness," colorblind ideology is a form of racism which promotes the idea that race is not an issue and racism can be alleviated by ignoring race.

Common Core State Standards Initiative: Initiated in 2010, the standards detail what K–12 students throughout the United States should know in core subjects like English language arts and mathematics.

The Cooperative Children's Book Center: A comprehensive site for information about young adult (YA) literature, especially multicultural literature.

Critical literacy: The process of "questioning a text" using questions that may reveal an author's bias, hidden agenda, or underlying messages.

Critical multiculturalism: Using critical or probing questions to question inequities in society.

Critical race theory (CRT):   CRT is a perspective about race and how racism operates in Western society.

Critical reading: The process of reading, analyzing, or unpacking a text for the purpose of understanding the author's point of view or claim.

Culturally responsive pedagogy: Teaching practices that view all students as capable of achieving at high levels.

Cultural tolerance: The respect and appreciation for culture.

Curriculum standards: This term refers to the academic standards and requirements put forth by the Department of Education. Each grade level has a set of standards.

Diversity: A range of human differences or unique traits that is not limited to race.

Formative years: The period of early childhood when emotional and social development is growing.

Frame of reference: A person's lived experiences become a major part of his frame of reference or set of criteria by which he learns to navigate the world and inform his daily judgments.

Heroification: The process of putting a person on a level where he is considered beyond human, infallible, and a hero.

Hidden curriculum: The recognition of how students are socialized and conditioned to accept hierarchical structures of power within and beyond the classroom.

Implications in research: The result of the study helps the researcher come to a certain conclusion that informs ideas or recommendations the researcher can share with the public.

Implicit bias: Feelings of which a person is not consciously aware. Biased feelings, which may be based on stereotypes, may prompt you to treat a person a certain way. A person's attitudes about a group of people.

Indigenous people: The inhabitants of an area who are known to be the first peoples in that area.

Message senders: People and things that provide information to us that we can then use to shape our understanding of others, events, and our surroundings.

Metric: A tool in research to measure data.

Monocultural curriculum: Curriculum, pedagogical strategies, and policies that represent the dominant culture. It reflects a dominant narrative embedded in the education system.

Multicultural education (ME):   A curriculum that challenges Eurocentrism, offering a viewpoint that is focused on intercultural awareness, and respect for diversity.

Multicultural materials: Materials that provide examples of multiculturalism and diversity.

Multicultural pedagogy: A "process of comprehensive school reform and basic education for all students which challenges and rejects racism and other forms of discrimination in schools and society and accepts and affirms pluralism."

Normalize multiculturalism: Celebrating multiculturalism in a way that makes multiculturalism a normal part of a system and not an anomaly or episodic.

Off color: Ideas, sometimes jokes, that are profane and in poor taste.

Protagonist in literature: The character named as the main character in the story who is usually a main component in the plot or conflict.

Psychic disequilibrium: This feeling occurs when a person of authority describes the world without you in it.

Public Broadcasting System: An American public broadcaster and television program distributor.

Racial consciousness: An in-depth understanding of the racialized nature of our world, requiring critical reflection on how assumptions, privilege, and biases about race contribute to a teacher's worldview.

Racial trauma: The distress people of color feel when subjected to racism or racially motivated violence.

Reader's journal: A notebook where a reader can write down his first impressions of a book or other thoughts about what he is reading.

Schema: Psychologists describe schema as pattern of thought that may dictate your behavior. When a person is thinking, his schema helps to organize his thoughts while involving his frame of reference to help him understand a concept.

Stakeholder: A member of an institution that provides the essential support needed for the institution to exist.

Systemic racism: Racism that is embedded in institutional or societal systems.

Task force: A group that forms for the purpose of focusing on a specific project.

Theory of mind: A social-cognitive skill that helps a person understand another person's point of view. Using this skill, and emotional intelligence, a person can consider the emotions, beliefs, and desires of another person. Theory of mind also inspires metacognition.

Universal theme: An idea about the human condition that any reader can connect with regardless of his cultural background.

US curriculum: The academic content and learning standards for each grade or academic level deemed necessary by the Department of Education.

Western canon: Literary works and other bodies of work in art, music, and philosophy held in high esteem.

White ally: A White person who takes an active stand against all forms of racism. Actively engaged in efforts to dismantle racist systems.

White backlash: The negative feelings that some White people express when talking about how race impacts our society.

White educational discourse: The way White teachers gloss over issues of race, racism, and White privilege that may reinforce the status quo.

White fatigue: When a White student expresses disdain for talking or learning about how race impacts our society.

White fragility: A phrase coined by DiAngelo (2011) that refers to a state in which even a minimum amount of racial stress becomes intolerable, triggering a range of defensive moves that "include anger, fear, and guilt, and behaviors such as argumentation, silence, and leaving the stress-inducing situation [which] function to reinstate White equilibrium."

White privilege: Opportunities or advantages that a White person can receive that may stem from systemic racism; protection from racism.

Woke: A person who is aware and actively attentive to the various forms of racism is said to "be woke."

References

Abdel-Fattah, R. 2007. *Does My Head Look Big in This?* New York: Orchard Books Publishing.

Aceves, T. C., & M. J. Orosco. 2014. "Culturally Responsive Teaching (Document No. IC-2)." University of Florida, Collaboration for Effective Educator, Development, Accountability, and Reform Center. http://ceedar.education.ufl.edu/tools/innovation-configurations/

Adam, H., & L. Harper. 2016. "Assessing and Selecting Culturally Diverse Literature for the Classroom." *Practical Literacy: The Early & Primary Years* 21, no. 2: 10–13.

Agirdag, O., M. S. Merry, & M. Van Houtte. 2016. "Teachers' Understanding of Multicultural Education and the Correlates of Multicultural Content Integration in Flanders." *Education & Urban Society* 48, no. 6: 556–82. doi:10.1177/0013124514536610.

Almasi, J. F. 1995. "The Nature of Fourth Graders' Sociocognitive Conflicts in Peer-Led and Teacher-Led Discussions of Literature." *Reading Research Quarterly* 30: 314–51.

American Association of Colleges for Teacher Education. 1973. "No One Model American." *Journal of Teacher Education* 24, no. 4: 264–65. doi:10.1177/002248717302400403.

American Library Association. 2009. "Attempts to Remove Children's Book on Male Penguin Couple Parenting Chick Continue." http://www.ala.org/ala/newspresscenter/news/pressreleases2009/aprll2009/nlw08bbtopten.cfm

American Library Association. 2012. "Coretta Scott King Book Awards—All recipients, 1970–present." http://www.ala.org/rt/emiert/corettascott-king-book-awards-all-ecipients-1970-present

American Library Association. 2014. "The Importance of Diversity in Library Programs and Material Collections for Children." http://www.ala.org/news/pressreleases/2014/04/new-alsc-white-paperimportance-diversity-library-programs-and-material

Apple, M. W. 1992. "The Text and Cultural Politics." *Educational Researcher* 21, no. 7: 4–19.

Ayala, E. C. 1999. "'Poor Little Things' and 'Brave Little Souls': The Portrayal of Individuals with Disabilities in Children's Literature." *Reading Research & Instruction* 39, no. 1: 103–07. http://hwwilsonweb.com

Bacon, J., & G. McClish. 2000. "Reinventing the Master's Tools: Nineteenth-Century African-American Literary Societies of Philadelphia and Rhetorical Education." *Rhetoric Society Quarterly* 30, no. 4: 19–47. Accessed August 4, 2020. www.jstor.org/stable/3886116.

Banks, C. 1996. "The Intergroup Education Movement." In *Multicultural Education, Transformative Knowledge, and Action: Historical and Contemporary Perspectives*, edited by J. A. Banks, 251–77. New York: Teachers College Press.

Banks, J. A. 2004. "Multicultural Education: Historical Development, Dimensions and Practice." In *Handbook of Research on Multicultural Education*, edited by J. A. Banks & C. A. M. Banks, 3–29. San Francisco, CA: Jossey-Bass.

Banks, J. A. 2007. *Educating Citizens in a Multicultural Society*. New York: Teachers College Press.

Barry, A. 1990. "Teaching Reading in a Multicultural Framework." *Reading Horizons* 31, no. 1: 39–48.

Bawagan, A. B. 2010. "Towards a Culturally-Relevant Pedagogy: Importance of Culturally-Sensitive Teaching Materials and Methodology." *Asia-Pacific Education Researcher* 19, no. 2: 185–97.

Bell, L. A. 2003. "Telling Tales: What Stories Can Teach Us about Racism." *Race, Ethnicity and Education* 16: 3–28.

Bernier, J. 2014. "Handbook of Critical Race Theory, edited by Marvin Lynn & Adrienne D. Dixson." *New Horizons in Adult Education & Human Resource Development* 26, no. 3: 71–73. doi:10.1002/nha3.20075.

Bidell, M. P. 2012. "Examining School Counseling Students' Multicultural and Sexual Orientation Competencies through Cross-Specialization Comparison." *Journal of Counseling & Development* 90: 200–207. doi:10.1111/j.1556-6676.2012.00025.x.

Bishop. R. S. 1997. "Selecting Literature for a Multicultural Curriculum." In *Using Multiethnic Literature in the K8 Classroom*, edited by Violet J. Harris, 1–20. Norwood: Christopher-Gordon.

Bishop, R. S. 2007. *Free Within Ourselves: The Development of African American Children's Literature*. Westport: Greenwood Press.

Bissonnette, J. D. 2016a. *Privileged Pages: Contextualizing the Realities, Challenges, and Successes of Teaching Canonical British Literature in Culturally Responsive Ways* (Doctoral dissertation). Retrieved from ProQuest Dissertations & Theses (10119821).

Bissonnette, J. D. 2016b. "The Trouble with Niceness: How a Preference for Pleasantry Sabotages Culturally Responsive Teacher Preparation." *Journal of Language and Literacy Education* 12, no. 2: 9–32.

Bista, K. 2012. "Multicultural Literature for Children and Young Adults." *Educational Forum* 76, no. 3: 317–25.

Blackburn, G., & T. Wise. 2009. "Addressing White Privilege in Independent Schools." *Independent School* 68, no. 3: 114–20.

Bolgatz, J. 2005. "Teachers Initiating Conversations about Race and Racism in a High School Class." *Multicultural Perspectives* 7, no. 3: 28–35. doi:10.1207/s15327892mcp0703_6.

Bonilla-Silva, E. 2010. *Racism Without Racists. Colorblind Racism and the Persistence of Racial Inequality in America* (3rd ed.). New York: Roman & Littlefield.

Botelho, M. J., & M. K. Rudman. 2009. *Critical Multicultural Analysis of Children's Literature: Mirrors, Windows, and Doors.* New York: Routledge.

Botelho, M. J., S. L. Young, & T. Nappi. 2014. "Rereading Columbus: Critical Multicultural Analysis of Multiple Historical Storylines." *Journal of Children's Literature* 40, no. 1: 41–51.

Boyd, F. B., L. L. Causey, & L. Calda. 2015. "Culturally Diverse Literature: Enriching Variety in an Era of Common Core State Standards." *The Reading Teacher* 68, no. 5: 378–87.

Boyer, J. B., & H. P. Baptiste. 1996. *Transforming the Curriculum for Multicultural Understandings: A Practitioner's Handbook.* San Francisco: Caddo Gap Press.

Boyer, J. B., & H. P. Baptiste. 2003. *Transforming the Curriculum for Multicultural Understanding: A Practitioner's Handbook.* San Francisco: Caddo Gap Press.

Boyer, P. G., & D. J. Davis. 2013. *Social Justice Issues and Racism in the College Classroom: Perspectives from Different Voices.* Bingley, UK: Emerald Group Publishing Limited.

Braa, D. 2016. "Critical Realism, Neomarxist Theory and Critical Pedagogy." *Radical Pedagogy* 13, no. 2: 9–32

Brooks, W., & J. McNair. 2015/1958. "'Combing' through Representations of Black Girls' Hair in African American Children's Literature." *Children's Literature in Education* 46, no. 3: 296–307. doi:10.1007/s10583-014-9235-x.

Brown, M. 2008. "Distinction in Picture Books." In *Considering Children's Literature: A Reader*, edited by A. S. Wylie & T. Rosenberg, 84–91. Buffalo: Broadview Press.

Burns-Bammel, L., G. Bammel, & K. Kopitsky. 1988. "Content Analysis: A Technique for Measuring Attitudes Expressed in Environmental Education Literature." *The Journal of Environmental Education* 19, no. 4: 32–37.

Butin, D. 2005. "Guest Editor's Introduction: How Social Foundations of Education Matters to Teacher Preparation: A Policy Brief Review." *Educational Studies* 38, no. 3: 214–29.

Butin, D. W. 2003. "Essay Review." *Educational Studies* 34, no. 1: 62–70. doi:10.1207/S15326993ES3401pass:[_]5.

Cai, M. 1994. "Images of Chinese and Chinese Americans Mirrored in Picture Books." *Children's Literature in Education* 25, no. 3: 169–91.

Carney, J., & C. Robertson. 2018. "People Searching for Meaning in Their Lives Find Literature More Engaging." *Review of General Psychology* 22, no. 2: 199–209.

Case, K., & A. Hemmings. 2005. "Distancing Strategies: White Women Preservice Teachers and Antiracist Curriculum." *Urban Education* 40, no. 6: 606–26.

Chafel, J. A., S. A. Fitzgibbons, L. Cutter, & K. Burke-Weiner. 1997. "Poverty in Books for Young Children: A Content Analysis." *Early Child Development and Care* 139: 13–27.

Chapman, T. K. 2013. "You Can't Erase Race! Using CRT to Explain the Presence of Race and Racism in Majority White Suburban Schools." *Discourse: Studies in The Cultural Politics of Education* 34, no. 4: 611–27. doi:10.1080/01596306.2013.822619.

Childs, D. J. 2014. "'Let's Talk about Race': Exploring Racial Stereotypes Using Popular Culture in Social Studies Classrooms." *Social Studies* 105, no. 6: 291–300. doi:10.1080/00377996.2014.948607.

Clark, A. N. 1969. *Journey to the People*. New York: Viking.

Cochran-Smith, M. 2000. "Blind Vision: Unlearning Racism in Teacher Education." *Harvard Educational Review* 70, no. 2: 157–90.

Cohen, L., L. Manion, & K. Morrison. 2007. *Research Methods in Education* (6th ed.). New York: Routledge.

Common Core State Standards Initiative. 2010. "Common Core State Standards for English Language Arts & Literacy in History/Social Studies, Science, and Technical Subjects." http://www.corestandards.org/assets/CCSSLELAStandards.pdf

Cooperative Children's Book Center. 2014. "Children's Books by and about People of Color Published in the United States." http://ccbc.education.wisc.edu/books/pcstats.asp

Creaser, W. 2010. "Crossing Multicultural Borders: Students, Faculty, and Difference in the University Classroom." *CEA Forum* 39, no. 1: 1–23.

Creighton, D. C. 1997. "Critical Literacy in the Elementary Classroom." *Language Arts* 74, no. 6: 438–45.

Crenshaw, K. W. 2011. "Twenty Years of Critical Race Theory: Looking Back to Move Forward." *Connecticut Law Review* 43, no. 5: 1253–351. http://archive.connecticutlawreview.org/documents/Crenshaw.pdf

Crisp, T. 2015. "A Content Analysis of Orbis Pictus Award-Winning Nonfiction, 1990–2014." *Language Arts* 92, no. 4: 241–55.

Cross, C. J. 2018. "Extended Family Households among Children in the United States: Differences by Race/Ethnicity and Socio-Economic Status." *Population Studies* 72, no. 2: 235–51.

Dei, G. 1994. "Afrocentricity: A Cornerstone of Pedagogy." *Anthropology and Education Quarterly* 25: 3–28.

Delgado, R., & J. Stefancic. 2001. *Critical Race Theory: An Introduction*. New York: New York University Press.

Devers, K. J., & R. M. Frankel. 2000. "Study Design in Qualitative Research 2: Sampling and Data Collection Strategies." *Education for Health: Change in Learning & Practice* 13, no. 2: 263–71. doi:10.1080/13576280050074543

Doll, C., & K. Garrison. 2013. "Creating Culturally Relevant Collections to Support the Common Core." *Teacher Librarian* 40, no. 5: 14–18.

Duke, N. K. 2000. "For the Rich It's Richer: Print Experiences and Environments Offered to Children in Very Low- and Very High-Socioeconomic Status First-Grade Classrooms." *American Educational Research Journal* 37, no. 2: 441–78.

Dyches, T. T., & M. A. Prater. 2005. "Characterization of Developmental Disability in Children's Fiction." *Education and Training in Developmental Disabilities* 40, no. 3: 202–16.

Edwardson, D. 2011. *My Name Is Not Easy*. New York: Amazon Children's Publishing.

Elo, S., & H. Kyngas. 2007. "The Qualitative Content Analysis Process." *Journal of Advanced Nursing* 62, no. 1: 107–15.

Escamilla. K., & S. Nathenson-Mejia. 2000. "Latino Children's Literature as a Tool for Preparing Teachers of Mexican and Mexican American Children." Manuscript submitted for publication.

Fasching-Varner, K. J. 2012. *Working through Whiteness: Examining White Racial Identity and Profession with Pre-Service Teachers*. Lanham: Lexington Press.

Fasching-Varner, K. J., R. E. Reynolds, K. A. Albert, & L. L. Martin, Eds. 2014. *Trayvon Martin, Race, and American Justice: Writing Wrong*. Rotterdam: Sense Publishers.

Flake, S. 2007. *The Skin I'm In*. New York: Jump at the Sun/Hyperion Paperbacks for Children.

Flintoff, A., F. Dowling, & H. Fitzgerald. 2015. "Working through Whiteness, Race and (Anti) Racism in Physical Education Teacher Education." *Physical Education & Sport Pedagogy* 20, no. 5: 559–70. doi:10.1080/17408989.2014.962017

Flynn, J. E. 2015. "White Fatigue: Naming the Challenge in Moving from an Individual to a Systematic Understanding of Racism." *Multicultural Perspectives* 17, no. 3: 115–24.

Follos, A. M. G. 2013. *Remarkable Books about Young People with Special Needs*. Chicago, IL: Huron Street Press.

Fondrie, S. 2001. "Gentle Doses of Racism: Whiteness and Children's Literature." *Journal of Children's Literature* 27: 9–14.

Fraenkel, J. R., N.E. Wallen, & H. H. Hyun. 2015. *How to Design and Evaluate Research in Education* (9th ed.). New York: McGraw-Hill Education.

Freire, P. 1973. *Education for Critical Consciousness*. New York: Seabury Press.

Freire, P. 1974. *Pedagogy of the Oppressed*. New York: Seabury Press.

Frequently Asked Questions: Common Core State Standards Initiative. New York: Distributed by ERIC Clearinghouse, 2015.

Gatimu, M. 2009. "Undermining Critical Consciousness Unconsciously: Restoring Hope in the Multicultural Education Idea." *Journal of Educational Change* 10, no. 1: 47–61. doi:10.1007/s10833-008-9087-5

Gay, G. 2002. "Preparing for Culturally Responsive Teaching." *Journal of Teacher Education* 53: 106–16.

Gay, G. 2013. "Teaching To and Through Cultural Diversity." *Curriculum Inquiry* 43, no. 1: 48–70.

Gillborn, D. 2006. "Critical Race Theory and Education: Racism and Anti-Racism in Educational Theory and Praxis." *Discourse: Studies in the Cultural Politics of Education* 27, no. 1: 11–32. doi:10.1080/01596300500510229

Gillespie, D. 2003. "The Pedagogical Value of Teaching White Privilege through a Case Study." *Teaching Sociology* 31, no. 4: 469–77.

Giroux, H. A. 1990. "The Politics of Postmodernism: Rethinking the Boundaries of Race and Ethnicity." *Journal of Urban and Cultural Studies* 1, no. 1: 5–38.

Glazier, J., & J. Seo. 2005. "Multicultural Literature and Discussion as Mirror and Window?" *Journal of Adolescent and Adult Literacy* 48: 686–700.

Gollnick, D. M., & P. C. Chinn. 2013. *Multicultural Education in a Pluralistic Society*. Columbus: Pearson Education.

Gordon, J. 2005. "Inadvertent Complicity: Colorblindness in Teacher Education." *Educational Studies* 38, no. 2: 135–53. doi:10.1207/s15326993es3802_5

Gorski, P. 2008. "The Myth of the Culture of Poverty." *Educational Leadership* 65, no. 7: 32–36.

Gough, D., S. Oliver, & J. Thomas, eds. 2012. *An Introduction to Systematic Reviews*. London, Thousand Oaks: SAGE.

Hall, K. W. 2008. "The Importance of Including Culturally Authentic Literature." *YC: Young Children* 63, no. 1: 80–86.

Haney López, I. 2006. *White by Law: The Legal Construction of Race*. New York: NYU Press.

Haviland, V. S. 2008. "'Things Get Glossed Over': Rearticulating the Silencing Power of Whiteness in Education." *Journal of Teacher Education* 59, no. 1: 40–54. doi:10.1177/0022487107310751.

Hawley, W. D., & S. Nieto. 2010. "Another Inconvenient Truth: Race and Ethnicity Matter." *Educational Leadership* 68, no. 3: 66–71.

Hayes, C., & B. Juárez. 2012. "There is no Culturally Responsive Teaching Spoken Here: A Critical Race Perspective." *Democracy & Education* 20, no. 1: 1–14.

Haynes, C. 2017. "Dismantling the White supremacy embedded in our classrooms." *International Journal of Teaching & Learning in Higher Education* 29, no. 1: 87–107, 21p.

Helms, J. E. 1994. "Racial Identity and "Racial" Constructs." In *Human Diversity*, edited by E. J. Trickett, R. Watts, & D. Birman, 285–311. San Francisco: Jossey-Bass.

Heewon, C., P. Soon-Yong, & C. Sleeter. 2018. "Multicultural Education: Using our Past to Build our Future." *International Journal of Multicultural Education* 20, no. 1: 1–4.

Hirsch, E. D., J. F. Kett, & J. Trefil. 1988. *Cultural Literacy: What Every American Needs to Know*. New York: Vintage Books.

Holland, K. F., & G. Mongillo. 2016. "Elementary Teachers' Perspectives on the Use of Multicultural Literature in their Classrooms." *Language & Literacy: A Canadian Educational E-Journal* 18, no. 3: 16–32.

Hollins, E. R., & M. T. Guzman. 2005. "Research on Preparing Teachers for Diverse Populations." In *Studying Teacher Education: The Report of the AERA Panel on Research and Teacher Education*, edited by M. Cochran-Smith & K. M. Zeichner, 477–544. Mahwah: Lawrence Erlbaum Associates.

Hood, S., & L. Parker. 1994. "Minority Students Informing the Faculty: Implications for Racial Diversity and the Future of Teacher Education." *Journal of Teacher Education* 45: 164–71.

hooks, b. 1989. *Talking Back: Thinking Feminist, Thinking Lack*. Boston: South End Press.

hooks, b. 1990. *Yearning: Race, Gender, and Cultural Politics.* Boston: South End Press.

Horning, K. T., M. V. Lindgren, & M. Schliesman. 2014. "A Few Observations on Publishing in 2013." CCBC Choices 2014. http://ccbc.education.wisc.edu/books/choiceintro14.asp

Hossain, K. I. 2015. "White Privilege." *Multicultural Education* 23, no. 1: 52–55.

Howard, G. R. 2006. *We Can't Teach What We Don't Know: White Teachers, Multiracial Schools* (2nd ed.). New York: Teachers College Press.

Hudson, J. 2014. "Breaking the Silence: Toward Improving LGBTQ Representation in Composition Readers." *Composition Forum* 29: 1–17.

Humes, K., N. A. Jones, & R. R. Ramirez. 2011. "Overview of Race and Hispanic Origin: 2010." U.S. Census Bureau. http://www.census.gov/prod/cen2010/briefs/c2010br-02.pdf

Iwai, Y. 2013. "Multicultural Children's Literature and Teacher Candidates' Awareness and Attitudes Toward Cultural Diversity." *International Electronic Journal of Elementary Education* 5, no. 2: 185–97.

Jackson, M., D. Green, L. L. Martin, & K. J. Fasching Varner. 2016. "Band-Aids Don't Fix Bullet Holes." *Democracy & Education* 24, no. 2: 1–6.

Jenks, C., J. O. Lee, & B. Kanpol. 2001. "Approaches to Multicultural Education in Preservice Teacher Education: Philosophical Frameworks and Models for Teaching." *Urban Review* 33, no. 2: 87–105.

Jensen, K. B., ed. 2012. "Grounded Theory." In *A Handbook of Media and Communication Research: Qualitative and Quantitative Methodologies* (2nd ed.), edited by K. B. Jensen, 329–33. New York, NY: Routledge.

Johnson-Feelings, D., ed. 1996. *The Best of the Brownies' Book.* New York: Oxford University Press.

Joseph, N. M., K. M. Viesca, & M. Bianco. 2016. "Black Female Adolescents and Racism in Schools: Experiences in a Colorblind Society." *High School Journal* 100, no. 1: 4–25.

Katz-Wise, S. L., & J. S. Hyde. 2017. "Facilitative Environments Related to Sexual Orientation Development and Sexual Fluidity in Sexual Minority Young Adults across Different Gender Identities." *Journal of Bisexuality* 17, no. 2: 141–71.

Kelley, J. E., & J. J. Darragh. 2011. "Depictions and Gaps: Portrayal of U.S. Poverty in Realistic Fiction Children's Picture Books." *Reading Horizons* 50, no. 4: 263–82.

Krippendorff, K. 2012. *Content Analysis: An Introduction to its Methodology* (3rd ed.). Thousand Oaks: SAGE Publications.

Kuby, C. R. 2013. *Critical Literacy in the Early Childhood Classroom: Unpacking Histories Unlearning Privilege.* New York: Teachers College Press.

Ladson-Billings, G. 1995. "'But That's Just Good Teaching!': The Case for Culturally Relevant Pedagogy." *Theory Into Practice* 34, no. 3: 159. doi:10.1080/00405849509543675.

Ladson-Billings, G. 1996. "Silences as Weapons: Challenges of a Black Professor Teaching White Students." *Theory Into Practice* 35, no. 2: 79–85.

Ladson-Billings, G. 2003. "Still Playing in the Dark: Whiteness in the Literary Imagination of Children's and Young Adult Literature Teaching." Paper presented at the NCTE Assembly for Research Midwinter Conference: Teaching and Researching across Color Lines, Minneapolis, MN.

Lamme, L. 2000. "Images of Poverty in Picture Books with International Settings." *The New Advocate* 13, no. 4: 347–64.

Lander, V. 2010. "Race, Culture and All That: An Exploration of the Perspectives of White Secondary Student Teachers about Race Equality Issues in their Initial Teacher Education." *Race, Ethnicity and Education* 14, no. 3: 351–64.

Landt, S. 2011. "Integration of Multicultural Literature in Primary Grade Language Arts Curriculum." *Journal of Multiculturalism in Education* 7: n.p.

Levitin, S. 1970. *Journey to America*. New York: Alladin Publishers.

Lieblich, A., R. Tuval-Mashiach, & T. Zilber. 1998. *Narrative Research: Reading, Analysis, and Interpretation*. Thousand Oaks: SAGE.

LiteraryDevices Editors. 2013. "Point of View." http://literarydevices.net/metaphor/

Logan, S. R., D. C. Watson, Y. Hood, & T. A. Lasswell. 2016. "Multicultural Inclusion of Lesbian and Gay Literature Themes in Elementary Classrooms." *Equity & Excellence in Education* 49, no. 3: 380–93. doi:10.1080/10665684.2016.1194239.

Lopez, G. R. 2003. "The (Racially Neutral) Politics of Education: A Critical Race Theory Perspective." *Educational Administration Quarterly* 39, no. 1: 68–94.

Lopez, I. H. 2006. "Colorblind to the Reality of Race in America." *The Chronicle Review* 53, no. 11: 62.

Louie, B. Y. 2006. "Guiding Principles for Teaching Multicultural Literature." *The Reading Teacher* 59, no. 5: 438–48. doi:10.1598/RT.59.5.3.

Manstead, A. 2018. "The Psychology of Social Class: How Socioeconomic Status Impacts Thought, Feelings, and Behaviour." *The British Journal of Social Psychology* 57, no. 2: 267–91.

Marianara, M., J. Alexander, W. P. Banks, & S. Blackmon. 2009. "Cruising Composition Texts: Negotiating Sexual Difference in First-Year Readers." *College Composition and Communication* 61, no. 2: 269–96.

Martin, M. 2014. "A Witness of Whiteness: An Autoethnographic Examination of a White Teacher's Own Inherent Prejudice." *Education as Change* 18, no. 2: 237–54. doi:10.1080/16823206.2014.907192

Masko, A. L., & P. L. Bloem. 2017. "Chapter 4: Teaching for Equity in the Milieu of White Fragility: Can Children's Literature Build Empathy and Break Down Resistance?" *Curriculum & Teaching Dialogue* 19, no. 1/2: 55–67.

Mathonsi, N. N., & N. N. Canonici. 2009. "Searching for the Thematic Element in a Literary Work." *South African Journal of African Languages* 29, no. 2: 109–20.

Matias, C. E. 2013. "On the Flip Side: A Teacher Educator of Color Unveiling the Dangerous Minds of White Teacher Candidates." *Teacher Education Quarterly* 40, no. 2: 53–73.

Matsuda, M. J. 1993. "Public Response to Racist Speech: Considering the Victim's Story." In *Words that Wound: Critical Race Theory, Assaultive Speech, and the First Amendment*, edited by M. J. Matsuda, C. R. Lawrence, III, R. Delgado, & K. W. Crenshaw, 17–51. Boulder: Westview.

May, S. 2003. "Critical Multiculturalism." In *Critical Theory and the Human Condition: Founders and Praxis*, edited by M. Peters, C. Lankshear, M. Olsen, & J. Kincheloe, 199–212. New York: Peter Lang.

Mayring, P. 2000. "Qualitative Content Analysis." *Forum: Qualitative Social Research* 1, no. 2: 5–56.

Mazama, A., & G. Lundy. 2013. "African American Homeschooling and the Question of Curricular Cultural Relevance." *Journal of Negro Education* 82, no. 2: 123–38.

McCarthy, C. 2005. *Race, Identity, and Representation in Education* (2nd ed.). New York: Routledge.

McIntosh, P. 1991. "White Privilege: Unpacking the Invisible Knapsack." *Peach and Freedom* 49, no. 4: 10–12.

McIntyre, A. 2003. "Making Whiteness a Topic of Inquiry in Teaching and Research." Paper presented at the NCTE Assembly for Research Midwinter Conference: Teaching and researching across color lines, Minneapolis, MN.

McKinney, K. D. 2005. *Being White: Stories of Race and Racism*. London, UK: Routledge.

McLaren, P. 1994. *Life in Schools: An Introduction to Critical Pedagogy in the Foundations of Education* (2nd ed.). White Plains: Longman.

NAACP History: W.E.B. Dubois. 2020. "NAACP. National Association for the Advancement of Colored People." https://www.naacp.org/naacp-history-w-e-b-dubois/

Neuendorf, K. 2002. *The Content Analysis Guidebook*. Thousand Oaks: SAGE.

Nieto, S. 1992. *Affirming Diversity: The Sociopolitical Context of Multicultural Education*. New York: Longman.

Nieto, S., & Bode, P. (2008). *Affirming Diversity: The Sociopolitical Context of Multicultural Education*. Boston: Pearson Education.

Nilsson, N. L. 2005. "How Does Hispanic Portrayal in Children's Books Measure up after 40 Years? The Answer is 'It depends.'" *The Reading Teacher* 58: 534–48.

Ninnes, P. 2000. "Representations of Indigenous Knowledge in Secondary School Science Textbooks in Australia and Canada." *International Journal of Science Education* 22, no. 6: 603–17.

Nixon, J. 2013. *Land of Hope*. New York: Delacorte Publishing.

Noguera, P. A. 2001. "Racial Politics and the Elusive Quest for Excellence and Equity in Education." *Education and Urban Society* 34, no. 1: 18–41.

North, C. E. 2009. *Teaching for Social Justice?: Voices from the Front Lines*. Boulder, CO: Paradigm Publishers.

O'Hare, W. 2011. *The Changing Child Population of the United States: Analysis of Data from the 2010 Census*. Baltimore: Annie E. Casey Foundation. http://www.aecf.org/KnowledgeCenter/Publications.aspx?pubguid5f667AADB4–523B-4DBC-BB5B-C891DD2FF039g

Olneck, M. 2000. "Can Multicultural Education Change What Counts as Cultural Capital?" *American Educational Research Journal* 37, no. 2: 317–48. doi:10.3102/00028312037002317.

Otsuka, J. 2011. *The Buddha in the Attic*. New York: Alfred A. Knopf.

Overstreet, D. W. 2001. "Organize!: A Look at Labor History in Young Adult Books." *The Alan Review* 29, no. 1: 60–66.

Özturgut, O. 2011. "Understanding Multicultural Education." *Current Issues in Education* 14, no. 2. http://cie.asu.edu/ojs/index.php/cieatasu/article/view/732

Pachankis, J. E., & Bränström, R. (2018). "Hidden from Happiness: Structural Stigma, Sexual Orientation Concealment, and Life Satisfaction across 28 Countries." *Journal of Consulting and Clinical Psychology* 86, no. 5: 403–15.

Parker, E. L. 2011. "Encyclopedia of African American Education (vol. 1 and 2), edited by Kofi Lomotey." *Teaching Theology & Religion* 14, no. 3: 297–98.

Patton, L. D., & J. L. Jordan. 2017. "It's Not About You, It's About Us: A Black Woman Administrators' Effort to Disrupt White Fragility in an Urban School." *Journal of Cases in Educational Leadership* 20, no. 1: 80–91. doi:10.1177/1555458916689127

Patton, M. Q. 2002. *Qualitative Research and Evaluation Methods.* Thousand Oaks: SAGE Publications.

Patton, M. Q. 2017. "Pedagogical Principles of Evaluation: Interpreting Freire." *New Directions for Evaluation* 155: 49–77. doi:10.1002/ev.20260.

Pedersen, A., I. Walker, & M. Wise. 2005. "Talk Does Not Cook Rice": Beyond Antiracism Rhetoric to Strategies for Social Action." *The Australian Psychologist* 40: 20–30.

Pence, D. J., J. A. Fields, A. Karpathakis, S. Parkinson, & L. Downes. 1999. "Teaching About Race and Ethnicity: Trying to Uncover White Privilege for a White Audience." *Teaching Sociology* 27, no. 2: 150–58.

Peters, M. A. 2015. "Why is My Curriculum White?" *Educational Philosophy & Theory* 47, no. 7: 641–46. doi:10.1080/00131857.2015.1037227

Philip, C. L., B. A. Dawson, & T. I. Burford. 2011. "The Complexities of Race and Ethnicity: Understanding Diversity in the American Context." *International Journal of Diversity in Organizations, Communities & Nations* 11, no. 3: 69–83.

Philip, T. M., M. C. Olivares-Pasillas, & J. Rocha. 2016. "Becoming Racially Literate about Data and Data-Literate about Race: Data Visualizations in the Classroom as a Site of Racial-Ideological Micro-Contestations." *Cognition and Instruction* 34, no. 4: 361–88.

Rice, P. S. 2005. "It Ain't Always So: Sixth Graders Interpretations of Hispanic-American Stories with Universal Themes." *Children's Literature in Education* 36, no. 4: 343–62.

Rich, A. 1986. *Blood, Bread, and Poetry: Selected Prose, 1979–1985.* New York: Norton.

Riley, C. A. III. 2005. *Disability and the Media: Prescriptions for Change.* Lebanon: University Press of New England.

Rose, D. G., & A. D. Potts. 2011. "Examining Teacher Candidate Resistance to Diversity: What Can Teacher Educators Learn?" *International Journal of Multicultural Education* 13, no. 2: 1–19.

Roue, B. 2016. "Subversion and Critical Distance: Black Speculative Fiction, White Pre-Service Teachers, and Anti-Racist Pedagogy." (Doctoral dissertation). ProQuest LLC.

Roughgarden, J. 2004. *Evolution's Rainbow: Diversity, Gender, and Sexuality in Nature and People.* Berkeley: University of California Press.

Saltmarsh, S. 2009. "'Depend on, Rely On, Count On': Economic Subjectivities Aboard 'The Polar Express.'" *Children's Literature in Education* 40, no. 2: 136–48.

Schniedewind, N. 2005. "'There Ain't No White People Here!': The Transforming Impact of Teachers' Racial Consciousness on Students and Schools." *Equity & Excellence in Education* 38, no. 4: 280–89. doi:10.1080/10665680500299668.

Schwartz, M., & M. Rogers. 2013. "Pew: Reading Habits Mirror Demographics." *Library Journal* 138, no. 2: 1–2.

Scott, D. M. 2004. "Postwar Pluralism, Brown v. Board of Education, and the Origins of Multicultural Education." *Journal of American History* 91, no. 1: 69–82.

Selvadurai, S. 1997. *Funny Boy: A Novel.* San Diego: Harcourt Brace.

Shannon, P. 2002. "The Myths of Reading Aloud." *The Dragon Lode* 20, no. 2: 6–12.

Shea, P. D. 2010. "Eliciting Picture Book Responses Up and Down the Grade Level Ladder, and Back and Forth across the Curriculum." *New England Reading Association Journal* 46, no. 1: 31–37.

Slaughter, R. A. (2019). *Summer Reading Lists in Private Middle Schools: A Qualitative Content Analysis of Multicultural Fiction.* Ann Arbor, MI: Proquest.

Sleeter, C. 1994. "White Racism." *Multicultural Education* 1, no. 4: 5–8.

Sleeter, C. 2018. "Curriculum Transformation in a Diverse Society: Who Decides Curriculum and How?" *Electronic Journal of Educational Research, Assessment & Evaluation* 24, no. 2: 1–11. doi:10.7203/relieve.24.2.13374.

Sleeter, C., & C. Grant. 1988. *Making Choices for Multicultural Education: Five Approaches to Race, Class and Gender.* Columbus: Merrill.

Soloman, M. 2002. "Content Analysis: An Opportunity for the Analytical Librarian." *Searcher* 10, no. 9: 62–67.

Souto-Manning, M., & J. Martell. 2016. *Reading, Writing, and Talk: Inclusive Teaching Strategies for Diverse Learners, K–2.* New York: Teachers College Press.

Stallworth, B. J., L. Gibbons, & L. Fauber. 2006. "It's Not on the List: An Exploration of Teachers' Perspectives on Using Multicultural Literature." *Journal of Adolescent and Adult Literacy* 49, no. 6: 478–89.

Starc, S., Jones, C., & Maiorani, A. (Eds.). 2015. *Meaning Making in Text: Multimodal and Multilingual Functional Perspectives.* London: Palgrave MacMillan.

Stemler, S. 2001. "An Overview of Content Analysis." *Practical Assessment, Research & Evaluation* 7: 1–6. http://pareonline.net/getvn.asp?v=7&n=17Document4

Stephens, M., & L. Phillips. 2014. "Social Class Culture Cycles: How Three Gateway Contexts Shape Selves and Fuel Inequality." *Annual Review of Psychology* 65: 611–34. doi:10.1146/annurev-psych-010213-115143.

Stevens, J. W. 2002. *Smart and Sassy: The Strengths of Inner-City Black Girls.* New York: Oxford University Press, USA.

Strauss, A., & J. Corbin. 1994. "Grounded Theory Methodology: An Overview." In *Handbook of Qualitative Research*, edited by N. K. Denzin & Y. S. Lincoln, 273–85. Thousand Oaks: SAGE Publications.

Strongman, R. 2005. "Development and Same-Sex Desire in Caribbean Allegorical Autobiography: Shani Mootoo's Cereus Blooms at Night and Jamaica Kincaid's Annie John and Lucy." *Kunapipi* 27, no. 1. http://ro.uow.edu.au/kunapipi/vol27/iss1/5

Sullivan, A. L., & E. A'vant. 2009. "On the Need for Cultural Responsiveness." *Communique* 38, no. 3: 8–9.

Swartz, P. C. 2003. "Bringing Sexual Orientation into Children's and Young Adult Literature Classrooms." *Radical Teacher* 66: 11–16.

Tan, Amy. 1989. *The Joy Luck Club*. New York: Putnam.

Tarca, K. 2005. "Colorblind in Control: The Risks of Resisting Difference Amid Demographic Change." *Educational Studies: Journal of the American Educational Studies Association* 38, no. 2: 99–120. doi:10.1207/s15326993es3802_3.

Taylor, L. K., & M. Hoechsmann. 2011. "Beyond Intellectual Insularity: Multicultural Literacy as a Measure of Respect." *Canadian Journal of Education* 34, no. 2: 219–38.

Taylor, M. 1981. *Let the Circle be Unbroken*. New York: Puffin Books.

Taylor, S. V. 2000. "Multicultural is Who We Are: Literature as a Reflection of Ourselves." *Teaching Exceptional Children* 32, no. 3: 24–29.

Terrill, M., & D. L. H. Mark. 2000. "Preservice Teachers' Expectations for Schools with Children of Color and Second-Language Learners." *Journal of Teacher Education* 51, no. 2: 149–55.

Tesch, R. 1990. *Qualitative Research: Analysis Types and Software Tools*. Bristol: Falmer.

The Annie E. Casey Foundation. 2010. "The Changing Child Population of the United States." https://www.aecf.org/resources/the-changing-childpopulation-of-the-united-states/

Thomas, E. E. 2016. "Stories Still Matter: Rethinking the Role of Diverse Children's Literature Today." *Language Arts* 94, no. 2: 112–19.

Thompson, A. 1999. "Colortalk: Whiteness and Off White." *Educational Studies* 30: 141–60.

Tropiano, C. 2008. "Paulo Freire, Social Change, and the Teaching of Gothic Literature." *College Quarterly* 11, no. 2: 12.

U.S. Census Bureau. 2012. "Educational Attainment in the United States: 2010—Detailed Tables." http://www.census.gov/hhes/socdemo/education/data/cps/2010/tables.html

Vlieghe, J. 2013. "Alphabetization as Emancipatory Practice: Freire, Rancière, and Critical Pedagogy." *Philosophy of Education* 185–93.

Warren, J. T. 2001. "Performing Whiteness Differently: Rethinking the Abolitionist Project." *Educational Theory* 51: 451–66.

Wasserberg, M. J. 2012. "'She Had a Caterpillar with her and Loved all Kinds of Slimy Things Normal Girls Would not Touch.' Combating Gender Bias with Nontraditional Literature in an Urban Elementary Classroom." *Networks: An Online Journal for Teacher Research* 14, no. 1: 1–9.

Wee, S., S. Park, & J. Choi. 2015. "Korean Culture as Portrayed in Young Children's Picture Books: The Pursuit of Cultural Authenticity." *Children's Literature in Education* 46, no. 1: 70–87. doi:10.1007/s10583-014-9224-0

Weekley, A. K. 2011. "Don't We All Want the Same Things?" *Transformations: The Journal Of Inclusive Scholarship & Pedagogy* 22, no. 2: 44–56.

Wiggan, G., & M. Watson. 2016. "Teaching the Whole Child: The Importance of Culturally Responsiveness, Community Engagement, and Character Development in Thompson, A. (1999). Colortalk: Whiteness and Off White." *Educational Studies* 30: 141–60.

Index

Abdel-Fattah, Randa, 83
Akbar, Naim, 61
Alexander, Melissa, 50
ally eyes, 37
American Association of College of Teacher Education, 2
American Journal of Education, 39
author's authority, 10, 89–111

background knowledge, 21
Backus, Megan, 73
Baldwin, James, 61
Banana Yoshimoto, 73
bias, 21
Birt, Marguerite Tiggs, 66
Black boy joy. *See* Black joy
Black joy, 77
bonding, 34
Bookbub, 63
Bookrags, 30
Bridges, Ruby, 53
Brown v. Board of Education of Topeka, 1
Buffalo Soldier, 41
Burton, LeVar, 55

Camp, Richard Van, 78
Capote, Truman, 74
The Cay, 15–17

Children's Book Council, 63
Cisneros, Sandra, 69
Civil Rights Movement, 38, 73
Clarke, John Henrik, 67
Collins, Addie Mae, 73
colorblind ideology, 19, 33, 112
colorblindness, 25
colored free schools, 66
coming-of-age, 70–87
common core state standards, 64
comprehensive school reform, 3, 113
The Cooperative Children's Book Center (CCBC), 19
core standards, 64, 112
Coretta Scott King Award, 72
Corsaro, William, 44
Counsell, Shelly L., 44
critical literacy, 12
Critical Race Theory, 33, 112
Cullen, Countee, 41
culturally responsive pedagogy. *See* culturally responsive teaching
culturally responsive teaching, 5, 112
cultural sensitivity. *See* racial sensitivity
cultural tolerance, 14
Curtis, Christopher Paul, 71–73

Department of Defense Education Activity (DoDEA), 64

dialogue. *See* discourse
discourse, 9
Diverse Book Finder, 19
diversity in YA, 63
Du Bois, W.E.B., 1. *See also* William
　Edward Burghardt Du Bois

Education and Urban Society Journal,
　39
Ellison, Ralph, 61
Epicreads, 63
equity pedagogy, 34
Euripides, 15

Floyd, George, 57
Freire, Paulo, 14
Fuller, Charles, 77

George G. Stone Center for Children's
　Book, 85
George Washington Williams, 1
Glaude, Eddie, 60
The Golden Kite Award, 72
Goodreads, 63
Greek dramatists, 7
Greenfield, Eloise, 85
Grimké, Angelina Weld, 77

Hansberry, Lorraine, 57
the hidden curriculum, 49
hooks, bell, 61
Hughes, Langston, 57

IJames, James, 77
implicit bias, 43, 89, 113
Indigenous, 14
The International Journal of
　Multicultural Education, 39
Islamophobia, 84–85

John Newbery Medal, 72
Jones, James Earl, 16
Juneteenth, 67

Kincaid, Jamaica, 80

King, Martin Luther, 53
King, Stephen, 74
Kuhar, Andrea, 55
Kunjufu, Jawanza, 61

Ladson-Billings, Gloria, 44
Lester, Neal A., 18
LGBTQ, 82
literacy events, 41

Maruno, Yoiko, 74
McBride, James, 57
McCoy, Elijah, 53
McIntosh, Peggy, 41
McNair, Denise, 73
message senders, 47, 49, 113
milieu, 17
Miller, Arthur, 77
monoculturalism, 14, 24, 50
multicultural curriculum, 34, 48, 89
multicultural education, 1–117

National Association for Multicultural
　Education, 4
National Association for the
　Advancement of Colored People
　(NAACP), 38
Ng, Celeste, 75
Nieto, Sonia, 44
No One Model American: a statement
　on multicultural education, 2
the n-word, 17, 67

Ohanian, Michelle, 59

Parents, Families, and Friends of
　Lesbian, Gay, Bisexual, and
　Transgender People (PFLAG), 63
physical handicap, 89, 91
Population Reference Bureau, 2
psychological, 44
The Public Broadcasting System (PBS),
　45

QUILT metric, 18–87

racial descriptors, 10, 109
racial sensitivity, 21
The Reading Quilt, 64
Reading Rainbow, 55
Recognition of Merit Award, 85
resource center, 27
Robertson, Carole, 73

segregation, 1, 67, 73, 112
sexual orientation, 20, 89, 91, 94
Shakur, Tupac, 41
The Sixteenth Avenue Baptist Church, 72
socioeconomic status, 50, 75, 76, 89, 91, 94
sociological, 43
Sophocles, 77
status quo, 33, 50
summer reading list, 25–38
systemic racism, 14

talking walls, 28
task force, 23–31
Taylor, Theodore, 15

teacher bias, 21
themes, 7, 28, 89, 91, 99
Thrasher, Max Bennett, 68

The Underground Railroad, 66
universal themes. *See* themes
US Census Bureau, 2

value gap, 60

Washington, Booker T., 67–69
Wesley, Cynthia, 73
Whitaker, Ronald W., 61
White fatigue, 35, 114
White privilege, 23, 25, 35, 41, 50
William Edward Burghardt Du Bois, 1, 38, 41, 60
woke, 35, 110, 114
Woodson, Jacqueline, 81–83
The World Health Organization, 79
Wright, Brian L., 44
Wright, Richard, 61

X, Malcolm, 61

About the Author

© Chelsea Slaughter

Rachel Slaughter is a reading diagnostician and currently serves as a learning specialist at an independent school. Dr. Slaughter received her BA in English communication and secondary education from Cabrini University, and MEd from Kutztown University. She received her EdD from Widener University where her research explores multicultural literature in private schools through the lens of critical pedagogy. Now entering her thirtieth year in education, she has taught in both secondary and higher education. After earning two fellowships and a distinguished track record of professional publications and presentations at regional and national conferences, she continues to write articles and blogs about multicultural education.